Just Mission

Just Mission

Practical Politics for Local Churches

Helen Cameron

scm press

© Helen Cameron 2015

Published in 2015 by SCM Press
Editorial office
3rd Floor
Invicta House
108-114 Golden Lane,
London EC1Y OTG

SCM Press is an imprint of Hymns Ancient & Modern Ltd
(a registered charity)
13A Hellesdon Park Road
Norwich NR6 5DR, UK

www.scmpress.co.uk

Scripture quotations are from the New Revised Standard Version
Bible, copyright © 1989 the Division of Christian Education of the
National Council of the Churches of Christ in the United States of
America. Used by permission. All rights reserved.

British Library Cataloguing in Publication data

A catalogue record for this book is available
from the British Library

978 0 334 05229 6

Typeset by Regent Typesetting
Printed and bound by
CPI Group (UK) Ltd, Croydon

Contents

Acknowledgements vi
List of Figures vii
Introduction ix

1 How Can Mission Be Just? 1
2 How Can Politics Be Practical for the Local Church? 11
3 What Is the Burning Issue? 29
4 Building the Team 39
5 Building the Case for Change 49
6 Engaging with the Christian Tradition 59
7 Identifying Who You Need to Speak to and What You Will Ask 68
8 Making Contact 80
9 Amplifying Your Voice 93
10 Evaluating Your Impact 104

Conclusion: Being Changed as Well as Seeking Change 111
Appendix 1 Being Political while Staying within the Law 117
Appendix 2 Working with Denominations and Agencies 121
Appendix 3 Reading the Book in a Small Group 123
Appendix 4 Further Reading 126
Bibliography 130
Index of Authors 135
Index of Subjects 137

List of Figures

Figure 1 Stakeholders in policy-making   21
Figure 2 Policy cycle   22
Figure 3 Policy cycle in reality   23
Figure 4 Justice-seeking cycle   29
Figure 5 Political cycle   87

Table 1 The distribution of discretion   71

Acknowledgements

Leading the Public Affairs Unit of the Salvation Army has given me the chance to work with enthusiastic and knowledgeable colleagues from whom I have learned a great deal. It is an immense privilege to represent the front-line work of the Salvation Army and to have as colleagues the headquarters teams that provide support. It is also a joy to have ecumenical colleagues with whom one can collaborate and who take a range of approaches to public affairs work that I feel complement one another.

This book has been written during a busy time professionally, and so I have needed two periods of round-the-clock support to focus on writing, one courtesy of Woodbrooke Quaker Study Centre and the other courtesy of my husband.

At a key moment in the writing of the book, I was able to share some of my work with the Professional Doctorate in Practical Theology Summer School. Being interviewed by Stephen Pattison helped to confirm my commitment to be a practising practical theologian.

I am grateful to two readers who read and commented on the whole text. Needless to say the responsibility for what has emerged is mine.

My thanks to Graham Stacey for the diagrams and cover and to Phil Coull for the indexes. I appreciate the collaborative way of working of SCM Press, and in particular Natalie Watson, who is a great source of encouragement.

Introduction

This book is written to act as a catalyst for local churches that are coming across examples of injustice and want to do something about it. It challenges local churches to read the signs of the times in their community and act upon their concerns in a way that will bring about change.

I am writing both for those who feel impotent in the face of injustice and those who are unsure whether the Church should have anything to do with politics. I will argue that mission and justice cannot be separated. I want to show how small 'p' politics can be a practical activity for the local church.

Reading the context

The period of austerity triggered by the financial crisis of 2008 has moved many churches to a compassionate response that gives direct and practical help to their neighbours in need. This response has taken many forms but includes things like debt advice, job clubs, community cafes and food banks. Social action projects have always been part of the life of the local church but there is a fresh sense of urgency about meeting need.

Over the last decade a new and innovative wave of evangelization has led many local churches to build relationships with those who have no faith or whose faith is nominal. In the Roman Catholic tradition there have been new groups formed around particular devotional practices or liturgies (Sweeney et al. 2006). In the Anglican and Free Church traditions new forms of church called 'fresh expressions' and 'emerging churches' have engaged with people through a shared cultural identity rather than a particular place (Shier-Jones 2009). The numbers of diaspora churches have increased rapidly, often with an intention of evangelizing their neighbours (A. Rogers 2013). These new relationships, initiated through evangelization, have increased understanding of the way people live and the joys and sorrows of their lives.

A growing number of churches are offering chaplaincy to local secular institutions who value a pastoral presence at the heart of their work. This has included chaplaincy to shopping centres, sports teams, residential homes, as well as local schools and colleges (Slater 2015).

What these changes to the mission of the local church have in common is that they have led to a greater understanding of the reality of ordinary people's lives and the way that the services and systems they rely upon can either support or frustrate them in their desire to live well. An example would be groups, like Street Pastors,[1] that provide pastoral care to young people enjoying the night-time economy. An older generation of Christians has learned about the lives of young people who might not usually come into their church buildings.

So developments in social action, evangelization and chaplaincy have, for many local churches, intensified their awareness of the lives of their neighbours and made friends of those who would formerly have been strangers to the life of the church. Church members have also become aware of the impact of austerity through their own working lives, families and volunteering.

The social structures within which we live are changing. Whether you think of health, education, employment, utilities, welfare benefits, housing or the other things we rely upon, the systems that make them happen have become increasingly complicated and fragmented. Sometimes it is unclear whether a problem is due to incompetence or lack of resources or whether a whole group of people is being disadvantaged by an unfair system.[2] While some organizations are highly responsive, it

---

1 See www.streetpastors.org.

2 Throughout the book I use the terms services, systems and structures to refer to those aspects of society that people come to rely upon but in which injustice

can often feel that the effort involved in sorting things out is exhausting.

It can be easy to forget that we live in a democratic society where at the end of the day, every significant system that people rely upon should be ultimately accountable to a politician. If it is a public service, no matter who delivers it, if the funding is coming from government, there is political accountability. If it is something delivered by a private company or a charity, then there should be some regulation in place and recourse for unfair treatment. In the final resort, there is the tribunal and legal system. In a democratic society there should be somewhere for frustration to express itself and seek justice.

It is a strange paradox that as anxieties grow about war and violence in countries that do not have democratic governance, so engagement with our own democratic processes continues to wane (Stoker 2006). Trust in politicians is low and so there is apathy about what democracy can deliver. For some people that apathy has turned to anger and people are joining political parties that resist 'politics as usual'. Many Christians will feel they have a responsibility to vote but will not feel that alongside that there is a responsibility to hold to account those who have been elected as their representatives. My analysis is that it is not that democracy has been tried and found wanting; it is that we have stopped trying to engage with it.[3] While the anger may be alarming, it is a signal that some form of democratic renewal is needed and so a call to engagement.

There are reasons for the apathy and the anger (Stoker 2006). Most of our knowledge of politics is mediated to us by the media. Anything that is dysfunctional or corrupt or self-serving is highlighted, giving the impression that this forms the majority of political engagement. A popular genre within reality TV

---

can become embedded. For example, when we go to the doctor we expect to receive a good *service*. We understand that the doctor's surgery is part of a complicated health *system* connecting hospitals, clinics and specialists. The health system also has *structures* that govern the flow of resources and accountability. All need to work together to deliver effective health care.

3 With apologies to G. K. Chesterton: 'The Christian ideal has not been tried and found wanting; it has been found difficult and left untried.'

suggests that every beneficial social system is being exploited and undermined by large numbers of people, which is a mis-representation of reality (Hills 2015). Little of the huge volume of 'human interest' media we consume contains reflections on the services, systems and processes that contributed to suffering or injustice. This makes it possible to read human experience as individual misfortune or good luck. Membership of the main political parties is at an all-time low, so many people do not know anyone who is politically active (Keen 2014). All this can contribute to a sense that engagement is likely to be futile.

Changing democracy

There are three important changes to democracy taking place that make the involvement of local churches in practical politics urgent if we are to inhabit a just society.

First, there is the growing devolution and localization of power. This means that the services and systems we rely upon may be different from one place to another and that import-antly the way in which they interact may also be different. It is good that decisions that matter to citizens are made closer to where they live, but it places greater responsibility on local citizens to hold those they elect locally to account. Justice will need to be established locally by people who are knowledge-able about their area and care whether or not it flourishes. This development of localism is often described as 'a postcode lottery', suggesting that no due process has taken place that resulted in those local differences. This is rarely true. It is more common that no scrutiny of those decision-making processes has taken place, meaning that unjust outcomes have not been challenged. Local churches have an honourable history of being interested in 'the way things are round here' and persisting in that interest over decades.

Second, there is the ever-increasing complexity of the way in which the services and systems we rely upon are organized. In the past, a letter to your Member of Parliament could be relied upon to get things moving but today it can often take some detective work to find out who is responsible, what discretion they have to change things and who they are accountable to. Often those individuals or voluntary projects that are most dependent upon services and systems working well are those with least resources to do the detective work. Local churches can be a valuable source of people who are able and willing to get to grips with complexity, and this book aims to give some pointers for that task.

Third, there is the period of intense legislative and regulatory change that has taken place in the UK since 2010 and whose consequences will become apparent over the next decade. Most of the major services and systems that ordinary citizens rely upon have been subject to legislative or regulatory change as a result of the Coalition government.[4] There is always a time lag between legislation and implementation and a further lag before the implications of implementation become apparent. When so many major social systems have been changed at the same time, there are bound to be new problems that arise from the way in which they interact with each other. Over the next five years, as the implications of these changes work through, there will need to be people taking a detailed interest in what works for the common good and what diminishes human flourishing. Because of the increasing devolution of power, that scrutiny will need to be done at local level. Where those people are Christians seeking justice they will want to use their knowledge to hold people to account.

One of the democratic achievements of which UK citizens are most proud is the welfare state that ensures a level of service in health, education, housing, social security and pensions that everyone can rely upon. In addition, the welfare state is seen

---

4 Schools, university funding, what health services are provided and by whom, welfare to work services, probation services, welfare benefits system, pension system, provision and funding of care for older people and disabled people to name just the most prominent examples. In addition, cuts to government spending mean that some services have been cut or closed, for example youth services and careers services.

as providing a safety net for those who fall on hard times and need support to deal with problems such as illness, disability, frailty in old age, and the costs of bringing up children, loss of work or loss of home. Now, elements of that support vary from place to place and so seeing who falls through the safety net and why is a task that local people need to undertake. Key responsibilities remain with central government and they too need scrutiny, but their work interacts with local arrangements and it is those details that comprise the reality of peoples' lives.

If local churches want to live in just communities, their democratic engagement is vital. They already bring important things to this task:

- a commitment to justice and human flourishing drawn from the Christian tradition;
- a long-term commitment to and involvement with their locality, its residents and institutions;
- an ability to understand and participate in complex structures, if they are active in the affairs of their denomination, for example;
- a diversity of skills and experiences and a willingness to work together either within their local church or across a number of local churches and agencies to achieve shared purposes.[5]

Some local churches already have individuals or groups pursuing a justice agenda sometimes with a focus on the developing world and sometimes with a focus on national campaigns. This book aims to persuade these seekers after justice that their passion and skills also need to be used on their doorstep.

---

5 Academics interested in the capacity of local churches have talked about their social capital, religious capital and spiritual capital, emphasizing that know-how and local relationships are an asset and that churches already have ways of building relationships beyond the local (Baker 2007).

What is the purpose of this book?

In summary, this book has three main purposes:

1 To give local churches a means of developing their desire for justice and acting upon it.
2 To encourage those preparing for and already engaged in ministry to become bolder in their public role.
3 To present the local church as an important location for the practice of small 'p' politics and so as a place where political and public theology will develop.

Who is this book for?

Local churches are the first audience for this book. I want to affirm the work for justice that is already taking place (see Appendix 2), embolden those who feel that something more needs to be done and inspire those who have not yet grasped the vision of politics as a practical proposition. In Chapter 4 I suggest that local churches have a mix of people but that work for justice draws upon those who start by asking 'Why is this the case?' rather than those who start by asking 'How can we help?' Together they make for a powerful combination when coordinated as different members of the body of Christ.

The second audience is those training for ministry or undertaking professional development. Most denominations now have many forms of authorized ministry both for ordained and lay people for which some form of training is required. That training usually emphasizes knowledge of the Christian tradition and the skills required to lead worship, provide pastoral care, teach the faith, enable mission and ensure good order in the life of the church. It can sometimes be overlooked that, in taking on an authorized ministry, a Christian is also becoming a public representative of the Church, which carries both responsibilities and expectations. I hope this book will encourage people in this position to reflect upon their public role and how it might be undertaken. As with all forms of ministry these days, the emphasis is on collaboration and participation (Heywood 2011).

My third audience is those studying practical theology. Practical theology is developing in many exciting directions at the moment. It is engaging with the concerns of the Church and the world; it is finding different ways of engaging with the Christian tradition and is being made accessible at many different educational levels. For me an important unifying element in practical theology is its ability to make connections between the pastoral, the practical and the political (Cameron 2012). I hope this book will enable students of practical theology to continue to make those connections. Appendix 4 offers some further reading.

Why have I written the book?

Four years ago I moved from an academic role in practical theology, directing the Oxford Centre for Ecclesiology and Practical Theology, to a practitioner role as Head of Public Affairs for the Salvation Army. With a small team, I am responsible for promoting and defending the work of the Salvation Army with policy-makers and politicians in the interests of greater social justice for those we serve. I moved from a role in an Anglican theological college, which was rightly preoccupied with preparing people for ministry and mission in the local church. Reflecting on my move I developed a concern that in its preoccupation with mission, the local church may miss the God of justice and the human injustice that is under its nose. I now have a real sense of urgency that the systems and structures people rely upon are being localized and that the local church needs to embrace this as part of its concern for the welfare of its community.

I realize that some people who pick up this book will be doing this already and I hope that the book acts as a source of encouragement and ideas. But I also want the book to open up a conversation with people who have genuine doubts about what I propose. The doubts most frequently expressed to me are these.

- It is not the job of the local church to interfere in people's lives.
- There are professional campaigning organizations that would do this better than us.
- We might look stupid if it all gets too complicated, or if it gets picked up by the local media.
- The political system is broken, and so there is no point trying to make things better.

I try to address some of these objections in Chapter 2. My experience has been that most politicians and policy-makers want to make things better and that what they often lack is authentic local feedback on how things are or are not working. That has come as a surprise to me because previously my view of such people came from the media rather than direct contact. I have made mistakes, and I have, on occasion, felt stupid, but that has felt pretty insignificant compared to the injustices experienced by the people my colleagues are serving. This book tries to convey some of the 'professional knowledge' I have acquired. However, I have also been able to recycle skills I have developed in other roles, such as asking questions, being organized, being persistent and building relationships. Local churches already seem well blessed with these skills.

I genuinely believe there is room for a range of approaches to justice-seeking by the broad spectrum of Christianity we have in the UK. It has been a great delight to work alongside public affairs professionals in other denominations and learn about their approaches (see Appendix 1). My aim in this book is to add another approach that I believe meets the needs of this moment as democracy is reshaped before our eyes.

How to use this book

I have written this book and now it is in the hands of the reader to decide what to do with it. However, I have designed it to facilitate three approaches.

Many local churches have small groups meeting for study and prayer, and in some places ecumenical groups come together in Lent (and at other times) for shared study. Appendix 3 offers a pattern of six meetings that could be used to work through this book. The case studies offer a thread through the sessions that can be used to test ideas as they emerge.

A common aspect of training for ministry is to have a placement and/or some form of project. I envisage that this book could be used to help someone engage in this aspect of ministry and reflect upon its contribution to their ministerial development. Increasingly training seeks to balance the academic classroom approach with active learning in a church or chaplaincy setting. The practical theology approach of this book aims to send us from practice to the Christian tradition and back to practice again.

In my book *Resourcing Mission* (Cameron 2010), I argued that starting with reflecting on what the local church actually does already is a productive starting point for mission. Asking questions about what we do and why we do it can produce new insights into what we really believe and then lead naturally into proposals for developing our practice. This book builds on that assumption. It affirms the social action, evangelization and chaplaincy practices of the local church and encourages the question, 'Why are things as they are?' This is the question that deepens the desire for justice and mobilizes those who have the gifts to be practically political. I envisage that one or two people in a local church or community could read this book and use it as a basis for setting up a team to do some practical politics.

Because the book is about a process as well as about justice, it is designed to be read in the order in which the chapters are presented. For those who prefer to cut to the action, it is possible to start at Chapter 3 and then loop back later to Chapters 1 and 2. There is a subject index to guide the person who might just be writing an essay in a hurry, and an author index and bibliography for those who want to follow up the sources that have shaped my thinking. I reference sources by putting the author surname and year in brackets which can then be looked up in the bibliography. The author index tells you where else I have mentioned that author.

Structure

Chapter 1 explores the relationship between mission and justice and discusses how the pursuit of justice sits alongside the other practices of the local church. Chapter 2 aims to unpack what is meant by politics and the approach to power I take in this book. Chapters 3 to 10 outline the series of steps that can be used to take an injustice and pursue it. The steps in fact form a cycle, rather like the pastoral cycle used in theological reflection. Each time you work through the cycle you become better equipped to take up another issue. Specific practices are described in the spirit of practical theology, which sees God's self-revelation occurring through both action and reflection. Chapter 6 focuses on making the Christian tradition an integral part of these practices as well as the source of the passion that motivates them. The Conclusion looks at how mission changes those who have been sent.

Weaving through the book from Chapter 3 onwards are two case studies which illustrate how the book might be used. They are constructed from fragments that I have gathered in my own research, teaching and political lobbying. Any resemblance to any church you may have come across is totally unintentional. They are there to stimulate reflection and discussion, and, as in real life, they do not always follow the advice given in the body of the chapters.

I

How Can Mission Be Just?

The rise of mission in the life of the local church

The rise in the Church of ideas about secularization has led to a resurgence of mission as a concept relevant to every local church. Charles Taylor (2007) in his book *The Secular Age* argues that secularization has taken different forms, that of social institutions, of daily practices and of individual beliefs. While sociologists such as Grace Davie (2002) have argued that this level of secularization has taken place exceptionally in Northern Europe rather than other parts of the world, nevertheless it is a reality that most local churches recognize. They are living in a plural society where a number of belief systems, including some that are based upon science and humanism, compete to influence how we live. The political theologian Luke Bretherton (2010) has taken up this new plural reality and compared it to the exile of the Israelites in Babylon. The prophet Jeremiah writes to them and urges them to seek the welfare of the city even though it is not their own city of Jerusalem. By analogy he argues that local churches that recognize their society as a plural one, where Christian ideas do not dominate public thinking, should still seek the welfare of that society and take part in politics to further that end.

The book by the South African theologian David Bosch (1991), *Transforming Mission*, had a significant impact on theologians and the life of the Church, reminding them that mission was the work of God and that the Church was an agent of God's mission only in so far as it discerned and cooperated with God's intentions. In time, this shifted the language of ordinary local churches that might formerly have used the word mission to describe work they were raising money for in distant countries rather than their own activities. It has also led to a greater humility in looking at the agenda of the Church and not assuming that it is endorsed by God without further theological reflection.

Compassion, righteousness, justice: integrating mission

In this chapter, I argue that if mission is the work of God then it will bear the marks of God's character, in particular his compassion, righteousness and justice. It follows from this that the work of the Church, if it is in collaboration with God, will also carry that character. In the Introduction I outlined three significant developments in the life of the local church: first, a growing range and volume of social action serving our neighbour in need; second, a flourishing of new approaches to evangelization, creating relationships with neighbours who had formerly been strangers; third, an increasing use of chaplaincy as a form of ministry in which the church is a pastoral presence in secular institutions and settings. My reading of these developments is that they enact the mission of a compassionate and righteous God, caring for those in need and wanting to build right relationships between himself and his people.

I now want to suggest that these developments of the routine life of the local church also carry the seeds of justice as a further characteristic of the God who sends us in mission to our neighbours. Fortunately I am not alone in making this assertion. Let me take two books on mission from different parts of the Christian tradition that also make this case.

First, two Roman Catholic writers, Stephen Bevans and Roger Schroeder (2004), in their book *Constants in Context: A Theology of Mission for Today*:

[In the twentieth century] it became apparent that the mission of the church was to be involved not only in the alleviation of human suffering and exclusion but also in the eradication of their roots. Not only was the church to engage in the corporal works of mercy through charitable service, but it was also to be involved in human development, the practice and establishment of justice and the struggle for liberation. (p. 370)

Second, an Evangelical writer, Christopher Wright (2010) in *The Mission of God's People*:

The community God seeks for the sake of his mission is to be a community shaped by his own ethical character, with specific attention to righteousness and justice in a world filled with oppression and injustice. (pp. 93–4)

The integration of compassion, righteousness and justice into a single understanding of mission mirrors my vision of practical theology as being practical, pastoral and political. For some, the missional instinct is to mirror God's righteousness and build relationships. For others, the missional instinct is to meet needs in a practical hands-on way. What for many churches seems more difficult is to ask the question 'Why?' Why do relationships need repairing? Why do these needs exist? In exploring what lies beyond the interpersonal we soon come face to face with the political. Chapter 2 will open up that encounter.

The good society

Mission is not an end in itself. It has a purpose or *telos*, that the kingdom of God should come on earth as it is in heaven. Unsurprisingly, Christians have developed different and sincerely held beliefs about what a good society might look like (Sagovsky 2008). Some place an emphasis on freedom for the individual, family and organizations to pursue the purposes that they think make for a good society. Others place an emphasis on the welfare of every member of society and feel that those with resources should be taxed by the state to provide the services that will secure the welfare of those without resources. Another contrast is between those who feel that fairness consists of giving everyone the same opportunities, accepting that this will lead to different outcomes depending on how those opportunities are grasped; and those who feel that some people through no fault of their own start at a disadvantage and so need additional opportunities to help them achieve the same outcomes as those who start from a position of advantage. The UK has a long history of seeking to balance liberty and welfare in public policy but it is a balance that continues to shift. For example, the debate leading to the Scottish Independence Referendum in September 2014 contained arguments about whether the people of Scotland wanted a different understanding of social justice from that they perceived to be on offer from the UK government (Stoddart 2014).

There is even disagreement about how these differing perspectives are to be reconciled. Some would say that each society must choose a dominant approach and expect others to fit in with it; others that a range of approaches needs to be in dialogue to reach some agreement on the common good; others still that agreement is impossible and that conflict about what society we want is the best way of recognizing competing needs and demands (Williams 2012).

It is not surprising that with this diversity of views many Christians choose to sit on the sidelines and allow others to engage in this battle of ideas in the political sphere, acting as spectators and consuming accounts of the action through the media. This book takes a plural perspective, that it is not possible or desirable to impose a single world view on society but that there should be a vigorous debate in which Christians participate fully, being open about their understanding of their tradition and the conclusions it leads them to. There are Christians working with integrity from different positions and some are unlikely to be satisfied with the approach to justice-seeking taken in this book.[1] The next chapter will unpick the ideas that underlie these different positions.

Understanding human need

Questions of injustice often arise from seeing people whose needs are not being met or where needs are being met inappropriately. This leads to judgements about who defines needs (Dean 2010). Most commonly within services and systems run by large organizations judgements about need are made by professionals or experts referring to a body of knowledge in which they have been trained. This can be at odds with what individuals feel their need is, especially when that need does not fall into categories recognized by the experts. People and groups vary in their ability to express their needs, with those most capable of making demands often securing better services. There is also a tension between seeing needs as being measured by a fixed standard or by comparison with what other people have. This tension is most evident in definitions of poverty, with the official measure being a relative one that acknowledges that taking part in a society is more than bare survival. Some of the needs that arise from social participation are generated by the market, which creates new goods and services that become an accepted part of daily life. The Joseph Rowntree Foundation annual exercise, which asks the public to assess what a basic minimum standard of living is, reflects these social changes (Davis et al. 2014). Our understanding of need is shaped both by culture and the market and not just by biological survival.

---

1 Vic McCracken helpfully brings five authors taking different views of justice and puts them in dialogue. See V. McCracken (ed.), 2014, *Christian Faith and Social Justice: Five Views*, London: Bloomsbury Academic.

The local welfare state

My experience of watching the rapid changes in social policy over the last five years has convinced me that much of the work in challenging injustice needs to be done at local level, if it is to have real effect. This is because of the way in which every major area of social policy has been either relegislated or redesigned to give greater decision-making powers to local bodies or to contract out services to organizations whose lines of accountability are not always clear.

In the past, a conversation about whether a social tenant could keep their child in a preferred school even though they were moving to another part of the town, to facilitate the parent getting a job, could have been carried out by two local government officials working in two different departments of the same organization, often in the same building. Now it is more likely that the social tenant has a housing association as their landlord and that the school is an academy free from local authority control and so in charge of its own admissions policy. Ensuring that the needs of both parent and child are taken into account could require a more complex set of interactions between two entities, neither of which may have any obligation to cooperate with the other. Fortunately, many of those working in these organizations have an instinct to cooperate, but they primarily have to respond to the requirements of their own governing bodies when using their discretion (I. Newman 2014).

Some writers on public policy have argued that from the 1990s onwards we have moved from a system of government to a system of governance where the structures and services citizens rely upon are dispersed between organizations that are fragmented and not obliged to work together to solve problems (J. Newman 2005). This fragmentation has had consequences for the local voluntary sector. Some organizations have stepped in to solve problems left by this reduced level of public sector coordination. Others have won contracts to deliver services formerly delivered by the state and so have become themselves part of the local network of governance. The period of cuts in public spending since 2010 has seen many local voluntary organizations lose funding and capacity and even close. This adds to the variations between localities in what services and support are available.

The market is not slow to respond to the varying needs of communities. The period of austerity triggered by the 2008 global financial crisis has seen the discount supermarkets expand both their number of shops and their customer base. The greater caution of the banks in lending to customers for consumer purchases has led to a range of new financial institutions on the high street and the internet offering unsecured credit at high interest rates. The more dramatic difference in appearance between high streets in poorer and more affluent communities is just one representation of the way in which the market adapts to the changing fortunes of localities.

This book is a call to the churches in each community to take an interest in the pattern of local governance and how it develops so that accountability, which is one foundation of justice, can be exercised. The quality of the relationships between local organizations that secure the essentials of human existence – food, housing, utilities, education, income, health and transport – will play a significant part in the quality of life in their communities.

Giving greater discretion at local levels can be positive, if it is used flexibly to solve individual problems. It can be less good if it makes people uncertain that their entitlements will be delivered in a fair and timely way.

Holistic care

The social action projects of local churches are often started to plug a gap in the safety net of the local welfare state that has become apparent to a person or group within the church. Building upon the existing resources of buildings, kitchen, volunteers, finance and relationships, this web of resources is spun into something that catches those whose needs were not being met by their household or existing public or voluntary services. Invariably, church social action projects aspire to work with people in a holistic way. While they have identified a particular need, they seek to relate it to the income, housing, employment, education and health of the people they encounter. The project is usually delivered in a relational way that listens to people on their own terms rather than fitting them into pre-existing categories (Bickley 2014).

This type of service provision often succeeds in engaging people who for various reasons are wary of existing, more formal, service providers. This capacity can then make the project attractive to public and voluntary funders. Ironically the requirements for accountability these funders require to safeguard their reputations can result in the service they are funding becoming more like the formal services which have failed with the people they are seeking to reach. This means that there can be a cycle to the social action of the local church as informal projects succeed, gain funding, employ staff, formalize and float free of the church that initiated them. Once a stand-alone organization, they can sometimes flounder as the safety net of resources that the local church formerly provided for them is withdrawn.

Another aspect of local church social action is that it can be most present where it is least needed and least present where it is most needed. Local churches in poorer communities often have fewer resources than those in more affluent communities and so the seedbed of resources from which a project can grow is not as rich.

For many activists in church social action projects, the plugging of a gap, the provision of holistic care are themselves significant actions in challenging injustice. This book urges others in the church to ask 'Why?' about some of the injustices the social action project seeks to address.

Is there room for justice in the local church?

There are many calls on the life of the local church. The growing discussion of mission has intensified the expectations of those in ministry both from those they lead and from those who oversee their work. This can make the discussion of justice seem like yet another item on an overfull agenda.

What is distinctive about making room for justice is that it is like a mustard seed: once planted it grows. It takes one person to ask the question 'Why?' about a particular injustice to draw others to join them in asking the same question. Once asked, that question can become like the piece of grit inside the oyster shell; it cannot be left alone.

The rest of the life of the local church need do no more than make the asking of that question possible. It can cultivate the ground that means that the seed grows in fertile soil. Worship can enable the contemplation and praise of a God who in his very nature is just. Discipleship learning and catechesis can indicate those parts of scripture and tradition that show God's anger at injustice and the response he desires. Pastoral care can provide healing for life's wounds but can also listen with a second ear and ask why those wounds were inflicted. Hospitality and fellowship can be about building deeper relationships, where it is possible to talk about life as it is really experienced in the household, the workplace, the community and the global context. As has already been suggested, acts of compassion and service can be reflected upon for the needs they expose and the injustices that may underlie those needs. Finally, the Church in its witness testifies to grace and hope that flies in the face of the anger, denial and despair that injustice can generate.

If there is a commitment to threading justice through the existing life of the local church in due season, questions will arise. The questions that energize will bring together those willing to pursue justice. The rest of this book shows how this can be done in small and local ways, but ways that make a real difference.

The local church has huge advantages compared to many groups in doing this work. It is inter-generational and so takes the long view on issues. It is possible to ask not only, 'What can we achieve by next week?', but, 'How do things need to change for our grandchildren and their children?' The enduring nature of the local church means it can be persistent. If one person has to stand aside, another person is likely to step into their place. The local church is relational, and so it has the capacity to build trusting relationships with those it wishes to hold to account. Those in ministry are not naive about the messiness of life. They accompany people at their best and worst moments and so have a capacity to deal with reality. This hopefully also means that local churches are not afraid of failure. They do not expect every problem to be amenable to quick solutions and know that best endeavours do not always work. Their calling is to reflect the character of God rather than build a reputation.

This chapter has sought to make a case for seeking justice as part of the life of the local church. The next chapter asks whether engagement in politics is a practical proposition.

2

How Can Politics Be Practical
for the Local Church?

This chapter explores how politics can be a practical proposition for the local church. The first section looks at how the pastoral work of the local church has political implications and the spectrum of responses that can be made. The second section offers some theoretical ideas about power and policy that will help the reader decide on their own position and approach. Finally, the chapter will look at the different relationships to politics that local churches can adopt before advocating for an integrated mission approach which sees practical theology as emerging from and contributing to a local context (Bevans 2002).

The pastoral is political

Personal, household, organizational, community, national, global

In the previous chapter, the ways in which Christians have expressed their longing for justice were discussed. The link between compassion, righteousness and justice was made, suggesting that this links the practical, pastoral and political aspects of practical theology and the social action, pastoral care and justice work of the local church. In a complex society, injustice can arise at a number of levels. At an individual level, people may not get the support they need to lead a secure and flourishing life. People live in households and there may be problems that affect all the members of a household. Some injustices may be experienced as part of participating in an organization. To give some examples. A group of service users might find that an organization treats them less favourably than another group. A group of employees might find that an employer is treating them unfairly. A group of tenants may form an association to ensure good resolution of issues with their landlord. Households and organizations are located in communities, and this is a further level at which injustice may be experienced. Poor communities can sometimes be served less well with services and facilities than more affluent ones, and this can affect the life chances of people in those communities. Poor transport links can act as a barrier to some communities accessing further education, employment and cheap supermarkets. Churches are often keenly aware of the different life chances available to people in different parts of the world. People with family links to such countries may be sending remittances to relatives or be using other means to further the prosperity of those countries.

Most social institutions and service providers focus on the individual. However, many enduring human needs can only be addressed in the context of supportive relationships. For most of us, the household we live in is the most important source of practical and emotional support. About 29 per cent of households in the UK now have one person living in them, and that can make finding and sustaining supportive relationships more of a challenge.[1] The local church is an important institution that can offer supportive relationships to people on an ongoing basis to supplement or at times substitute for lack of immediate biological family. Local churches also view people as members of households and are concerned for the well-being of the household, even if only one member of it is involved with the church. This is a valuable complement to the individual focus that often dominates the world view of formal service providers. Local churches have often used the language of family

---

1 www.ons.gov.uk/ons/taxonomy/index.html?nscl=One-person+Households.

to describe households. We know that the cost and shortage of housing and the fragmenting of some nuclear families means that the reality is sometimes more complicated (Reader 2008). Some of the language used about the earliest churches in the New Testament talks about them as 'households of faith' bringing together diverse groups of people under the same roof but with a common desire for the well-being of all.

In setting out these different levels at which injustice may occur I want to emphasize that pastoral relationships, while grounded in the interpersonal, often give insights to injustices being experienced at the household, organizational, community and even global level. To know about these injustices is to ask why they exist and to encounter questions about decision-makers and how they use their power.

This insight is not new but it is not always accepted. It was the second wave of feminist writers and activists in the 1960s and 1970s who pointed out that although women's lives were largely lived in the domestic sphere, the things that concerned them nevertheless had political implications (Bennett Moore 2002). The struggle by some women to gain more prominent roles in the public sphere, including politics, was in part a desire to bring their concerns to public attention. In fact the separation between private and public spheres became seen as problematic in that it allowed some concerns to be dismissed as domestic and to avoid appropriate scrutiny. Thinking about the pastoral as both multi-levelled and connected to the political paves the way for asking questions about justice.

Inform, support, advise, advocate, lobby and campaign

Pastoral relationships make us aware of different levels of injustice. A knowledge of the agencies and services in our local community can make us aware of a range of possible responses to injustice.

At the most basic level, informing someone of the help available to them or the avenues of redress open to them can enable them to seek justice. In a complex world it is not surprising that people do not always understand how the structures and services they rely upon can be held to account and who might assist them in that process. Being well informed about such matters is an important first step.

Knowing that someone can help is very different from being able to access that help. For a whole range of reasons people can find that help-seeking step difficult. It can be practical difficulties such as the cost of transport, the physical accessibility of buildings or the need for translation. It can be emotional difficulties such as lack of confidence, worries about being able to present complicated information fluently or previous bad experiences of dealing with those in authority. Straightforward practical or emotional support can open up the possibility of redress that previously seemed impossible.

Information and support can soon spill over into advice and here it is worth stopping to consider whether you are sufficiently knowledgeable to give advice or whether referral to an advice-providing agency would be more appropriate. An example of this can be seeking to support someone with debt problems. There are many valuable ways of helping: informing them of online sources of help; helping them make use of a budgeting tool; giving them a lift to a debt advice agency; or providing emotional support to attend a first appointment. These are all positive. However, if you step over the line and offer advice which is taken and then means the person is financially worse off than if they had ignored you, this is to compound rather than tackle injustice. Thinking about where that boundary lies is important. If advice agencies have frustratingly long waiting lists, then that highlights an injustice at the community level which can lead to another important 'Why are things like this?' question.

In our own lives we prefer to speak for ourselves rather than have others speak for us. Many organizations that provide services for people with a difficulty or barrier to using the service provide them with advocates who can help them work out what they want and what steps they need to take to get it.

Advocacy support that enables someone to resolve issues in their own way and to their own satisfaction is preferable to taking the problem out of their hands.

When existing systems of redress to right an injustice have been exhausted, it will be necessary to progress to lobbying either to have the system or service changed or to get the discretion that is available to the decision-maker used more fairly. There are individuals and households who are capable of taking on this more ambitious task by themselves, but many people will find strength in solidarity with others in a similar position and in working as a group to challenge. It may also be discovered that local advice-giving agencies have insufficient capacity to deal with the volume of cases being brought to them, and this can in itself become a focus for lobbying. This book discusses practically how this might be done.

Identifying where the decisions are made is crucial in lobbying effectively and Chapter 7 spells this out in more detail. Local problems can usually be tackled locally but sometimes it is necessary to seek to influence national policies to bring about change. Where you are dealing with a local branch of a national organization, there may be insufficient discretion allowed locally to make a meaningful response.

Sometimes everything that has been discussed in this section fails to work and it is evident that pressure will need to be brought to bear on the organization to change its policies. The attempt to use external influence to shift organizational behaviour is known as campaigning and involves mobilizing public opinion in support of your cause. Chapter 9 will say more about this.

Justice-seeking can involve a range of activities but it focuses on those affected by the issue and what they are seeking.

Understanding power

Seeking justice is about asking why things are as they are, who has the power to change them and how that person or body might be effectively persuaded to right the injustice. For Christians to feel able to do this they need to give some thought to what they believe about power. This section looks at three ways of understanding power and four tactics for bringing about change, and finally discusses the relationship between authority and influence.

Unitary, plural, radical

There are three assumptions about how power works that can be found in the services, systems and structures that affect people. A unitary understanding of power assumes that all power derives from a single source and that it is distributed according to the authority of that single source. Conflict is seen as dysfunctional and needing to be resolved, if necessary by appealing to the next level in the hierarchy.

A plural understanding of power assumes that in any situation there will be different stakeholders with different sources of power who need to collaborate despite the tensions and conflicts that may occur. The diversity of the stakeholders and the conflicts between them are seen as positive and helping them to arrive at the best outcome for all involved.

A radical view of power assumes that there are structural inequalities in society so profound that any situation will be a conflict that cannot be reconciled. Conflict may be suppressed as decisions are imposed, but it will re-emerge as the incompatible interests of the unequal groups again become evident.

The mechanisms that can be used in justice-seeking will depend upon the assumptions about power. In this book, I take a plural view of power and so see merit in all four of the tactics described below and feel there is a place for all three perspectives on power. However, I have to acknowledge that is a very plural way of seeing things. For someone with a unitary view of power, only clear lines of accountability to an ultimate source of authority would safeguard the interests of the marginalized. For someone with a radical view of power, only system-wide change would be seen as likely to remedy inequalities and that change will only be brought about by resistance and rebellion. Reform, particularly small-scale reform, cannot work.

The word plural or pluralism is now used to mean many things, and so I want to clarify that here I am using it to mean the recognition that society contains different stakeholders and that these stakeholders may adopt different world views that need to be brought into conversation and, if necessary, respectful disagreement, if policy is to be developed. It is not the same as relativism, which suggests that all world views have an equal validity. Miroslav Volf (2011), in his book *A Public Faith: How Followers of Christ should Serve the Common Good*, explains religious pluralism as follows:

> Since truth matters, and since a false pluralism of approving pats on the back is cheap and short-lived, adherents of various religions will rejoice in overlaps and engage each other on differences and incompatibilities. (p. 131)

Rowan Williams (2012), in *Faith in the Public Square*, explains the role of the state in a plural society as follows:

> [Pluralism] denotes a self-awareness on the part of the state, a recognition that actual civil society is composed of a variety of groups with a variety of convictions and habits, moral and ritual, so that the state's task is to seek the best possible co-existence and interaction between them for the attainment of goods that no one group can secure alone. It denotes a recognition also that religious diversity is neither a problem to be overcome nor a threat to be controlled. (p. 135)

The way we understand power has implications for the actions or tactics we will use to advance an issue of injustice. I now move on to consider four tactics for influencing authority.

Affirm, reform, resist and rebel

Affirming what is being done well is the tactic that is most commonly overlooked in lobbying but that is frequently successful. It is rare (but not impossible) to find a service or system or structure that is totally without merit. To say what is being done well or what provides some measure of justice in the situation is helpful. It affirms those who work to deliver the service. It makes clear that redress is sought within the context of that which is positive. It provides bridges to build from what is happening now to what is desired. It is worth taking the trouble to give positive feedback about services that you or your community rely upon. It is not always evident what battles providers are fighting on behalf of their service users and unsolicited positive feedback can go a long way in showing that a community values the agencies that are there to serve it.

Legitimate authority should be open to reform or should at least be able to offer a reasoned account of why a proposal for reform is not being accepted. Where reform proposals are rejected then campaigning can be undertaken to mobilize public opinion in favour of the reform, giving it a competing legitimacy with the status quo. Much of this book explains how to formulate and make effective requests for change. It does not start from the position that such attempts are futile or that structures and agencies will refuse to give an account of their policies and actions. However, legitimate authority does not always respond in an accountable way and so further tactics may be needed to highlight the injustice to those responsible for regulation and funding or to elected politicians.

Where power is unamenable to reform it is possible to consider the options of resisting that power or rebelling against its requirements. However, it is important to consider the possible consequences of such tactics and whether those adopting them are fully able to deal with the consequences. Sometimes symbolic actions of resistance and rebellion can be staged as part of a campaign to draw the public's attention to the injustice that is being tackled. Carefully designed acts of resistance and rebellion can helpfully expose pettiness, rigid rules and unwillingness to listen to, influence or negotiate with stakeholders. They can also be used to demonstrate opposition to a status quo that does not wish to enter into dialogue. Chapter 9 will discuss these tactics further.

Authority and influence

In a democratic society most power has boundaries placed around it and can be described as authority and influence. Authority enables a group of people to work together in systems and structures to achieve work that is beyond the efforts of each individually. It creates an agreement as to the means by which resources are to be allocated and differences resolved. However, the authority is bounded by the purpose of the organization. A straightforward example is of a choir. The members agree that the conductor can coach and direct them in order to give the best possible performance, but they do not expect the conductor to advise them on where to go on holiday. It is the governance of an organization that links its purpose to its authority and explains to all involved in the organization how that authority will be exercised and held to account. In most contexts, this is done by a separation of powers whereby the governance structures hold the executive structures to account for achieving the purposes of the organization. If the primary purpose of a church choir is to enhance worship, its leader can be called to account if all its efforts are directed to fundraising, even if that is a desirable secondary purpose.

Authority can become insular and rigid if it is not open to influence from stakeholders. A conductor who takes no interest in choir members' views on what the choir is singing is likely to find a dwindling membership. However, while choir members seek to influence, they realize that a successful concert is not merely a collection of members' favourites, and so the conductor will need to exercise authority as well as being open to influence. Influence is vital to the responsive exercise of authority. However, to be legitimate, influence needs to be exercised transparently. If it is not openly known who has access to those in authority and what input they are making, then the interests of some stakeholders may be favoured over others and at worst the opportunity for corruption arises.

In any organization, system or structure, accountable authority and transparent influence need to become mutually interdependent. Some key questions that could be asked to establish this might include:

- What are the boundaries around this authority?
- How is this authority held to account?
- What are legitimate means of influencing this authority?
- How are the means of influencing kept transparent?

In seeking to influence authority, local churches need to think about their own transparency.

Understanding policy

There is a language that lies between citizens' experiences of services, systems and structures and the political decisions that shape them: it is the language of policy. Policy-making is the means by which problems are formulated, options proposed, decisions made and new ways of working implemented. Like all specialist languages, it can descend into jargon and give everyday words technical meanings. However, given the real impact that policies have on citizens, it is not unreasonable that they should be consulted in a language they can understand and should be able to make representations in plain English. This section explains who is involved in making policy and in the cycle of activities that shape it.

Policy stakeholders

Policy is not just the preserve of politicians and policy-makers;
a range of stakeholders influence it directly and create a climate
of debate by the way in which they interact with each other.

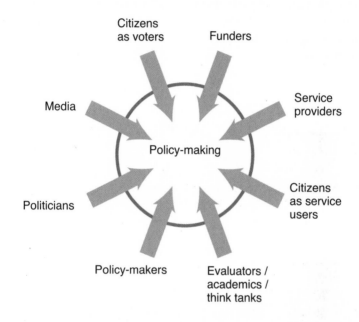

Figure 1: Stakeholders in policy-making.

Figure 1 indicates eight main stakeholders in policy-making.
In seeking to influence policy, all eight can be sources of information about a policy and also have their own perspective on
the effectiveness of the policy. It should be possible to identify
which stakeholders are likely to be allies in seeking change
and to decide when in a justice-seeking process to engage with
them.

Policy cycle

Classically the making of policy is described as a cycle with the following four elements, indicated in Figure 2.

1 Understanding the context.
2 Developing options.
3 Getting to decisions.
4 Making it happen.

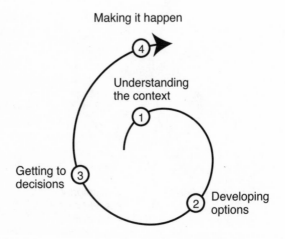

Figure 2: Policy cycle.

Michael Hallsworth and colleagues, in their report *Policy Making in the Real World* (2011), suggest that in reality this cycle intersects with three forces that can shape and deflect it: evidence, politics and delivery. The use of evidence in policy-making can seem like a holy grail with just one more fact making the way ahead clear. However, there are clearly some policies that work better than others and it would be foolish to ignore evidence that someone has a better solution to the problem. Policy-making can never become an activity reserved for experts because policy-makers derive their power from politicians and politicians have their own views about what works and are sensitive to voter and media views about what they should be doing. Indeed, it is their role to represent voters in the policy-making process, so it would be strange if they were excluded from it. Policies are designed to be implemented and so understanding the capacity of systems and structures underpins successful policy-making. Information about what is happening in practice can be influential at any stage of the process.

Crises and events often overtake policy-making especially when failure to deliver current policies creates a greater sense of urgency for change (see Figure 3).

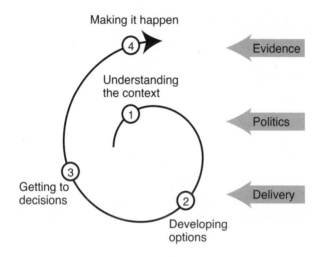

Figure 3: Policy cycle in reality.

Based upon their research into real policy-making, Hallsworth and colleagues go on to say that it is wrong to assume that a policy you are seeking to influence has a clear purpose that fits the real problem, or is well designed, or is based upon evidence rather than having had evidence assembled to support it. This may seem a rather bleak analysis and it would be foolish to suggest that major policy failures do not occur (King and Crewe 2013). However, it does suggest that there is scope at any stage in the policy-making process for citizens to speak up with their own evidence of the problem and ideas for its resolution, their own political views and their own experience of how delivery is working in practice.

Is there room for politics in the local church?

Unsurprisingly, Christians with different understandings of power take different views on the role for the Church in politics. This section summarizes four roles: example, guide, partner and radical challenge. It then proposes the integrated mission approach taken in this book. This is not to dismiss the value of the other approaches but to make room for one more in the complex task of enacting God's mission to the world.

Example, guide, partner, radical challenge, integrated mission

Example

Some theologians would be cautious about any direct engagement between the churches and politics. They would be happy for Christians to become politically active as individuals but not for the Church as an institution to have a voice. They would see the main role of the Church as acting as an example of the power relations that God seeks between people and in particular emphasize relationships that exemplify peace, justice and humility. Elaine Graham (2013), in Chapter 4 of her book on public theology gives a helpful account of the key theologians involved, grouping them into post-liberal theologians such as Stanley Hauerwas and radical orthodox theologians such as John Milbank.

Guide

This approach sees the Church as a source of moral and ethical guidance for society which is for those with authority to apply (Atherton et al. 2011). Jonathan Chaplin suggests, 'Political wisdom involves discerning how a body of political principle is to assume concrete form in policy-making and statesmanship at a particular time and place' (2009, p. 211). Based upon his reflections on the contributors to the book, Chaplin then goes on to propose three core principles:

- Government is created, fallen and open to redemption.
- Government is legitimate, limited, accountable, diffused and representative.
- Government is established to secure justice and the common good (see pp. 212–30).

Conversations between theologians and policy-makers will help unpack the implications of these principles for policy. A recent edited collection by Malcolm Brown (2014), *Anglican Social Theology*, explores how this approach has developed.

Partner

Community organizing involves local churches as a community partner working with others to campaign. It is active in London and five other UK cities. Ritchie et al. offer a helpful explanation of what this involves:

> Community organizing involves building an alliance of religious congregations, schools and civic associations to work together on issues of common concern. It seeks to build a 'relational culture': encouraging people to share their stories, and identify the ways in which their areas can be changed for the better. When people are in relationship, with common concerns, they are in a position to challenge those with the power to deliver change (be that environmental

improvements, better pay for workers, or improved public services). While the campaigns are on specific, winnable issues, the wider aim is to build a local and national alliance with an ongoing set of relationships of trust and commitment – where each successful campaign not only brings a tangible result (such as improved social housing, or higher wages) but develops grassroots leadership and the power of people in Britain's poorest neighbourhoods to work together for the common good. (2013, p. 19)

There is a growing literature describing and reflecting upon this approach (Bretherton 2010; Ivereigh 2010; Shannahan 2014).

Radical challenge

Another group of authors speak from a radical perspective. For some this involves incarnational mission, an intentional living alongside those who are systematically marginalized and acting with them in their interests (Bishop 2007; Thomas 2013). In his account of two fresh expressions of church in Bradford, Chris Howson (2011) shows how principles of liberation theology have been used to develop their work. One of the conclusions he reaches is that the Church should see protest as mission. 'The Church must be a visible presence within movements to build a fairer and more just society ... Whenever we protest, we make visible God's desire for a better world' (p. 132). In a chapter called 'Re-imagining the Systems', Hebden (2013), also writing from a radical perspective, says, 'We must understand how the privileged minority keep the working majority in controlled and subdued limits. Our imaginations have become hostage to the imaginings of the powerful' (p. 25).

Integrated mission

This book takes an integrated mission approach seeing the Church as already involved in the messy reality of people's lives and asking justice-seeking questions from that involvement.

That involvement makes the search for small-scale reform worth the risk of failure, if it tackles the details that make such a difference to human flourishing. The involvement in detail can help hold to account the services, systems and structures that shape people's lives and that, if they go unchallenged, can lose their focus on the citizens they are intended to serve. This approach tackles power, rather like the elephant in the room, a small piece at a time, while learning how to contribute to the bigger picture of whether or not democracy is in good health.

Putting democracy to the test

Democracy relies upon citizens both voting and holding their elected representatives to account. The centralized state that evolved in the UK during and since the Second World War has led many people to assume that the 'holding to account' was being done by experts or the media and required no specific action on their part.

As a more decentralized democracy emerges, the question of who holds politicians to account is being reopened. The devolution of some political powers to Scotland, Wales and Northern Ireland has created awareness that different powers are held in different places and so accountability needs to be brought to bear in different ways. The greater moves to localism that have taken place since 2010 and look set to continue after the May 2015 general election mean that local politicians will have greater powers and will need holding to account locally. The greater involvement of private companies and voluntary organizations in delivering services we rely upon means they too must be held to account. The remaining chapters of this book show how, in practice, local churches can get involved in this holding to account.

Seeing things differently and staying in fellowship

As individuals, we vary greatly in our personal reactions to conflict. Some people feel uncomfortable at the hint of a mild disagreement, other people 'enjoy a good scrap' and feel that conflict adds spice to life. To engage in practical politics is to embrace the possibility of conflict within the team, between the team and its stakeholders, and between the team and those with the authority to change things. As a matter of pastoral concern, it is good for team members to become familiar with each other's personal response to conflict. Those who feel reasonably resilient in situations of conflict might offer to undertake those presentations and meetings where some conflict can be anticipated.

Diversity is a strength in a team as it allows an issue to be examined from a range of perspectives. However, working with others different from ourselves can uncover assumptions about life in general, and how to do things in groups in particular, of which we were unaware. It is good to talk these assumptions through with a trusted friend or spiritual adviser to see whether they are firmly held principles or habitual ways of working that could be amended.

However, there are likely to be disagreements about aims and approach within the team from positions of integrity. I hope this chapter has given some means of discussing what the source of these disagreements might be and whether there remains a sufficiently common mind to proceed together. Some will find it easier than others to set aside a personal position in order to further the work of the team. No one should feel pushed to a point that they feel they cannot in conscience sustain. Learning to disagree and part company but stay in fellowship is a mark of holding the diversity of the Church, which aspires to, but has not yet fully reached, unity.

3

What Is the Burning Issue?

This chapter begins the sequence of eight chapters that enable you to work through an issue of injustice as a matter of practical politics. If you read the chapter titles, you will see that they set out a series of steps that can be taken to raise a question of injustice and ask for change. It may be that on completing the steps the issue is resolved to everyone's satisfaction. It is also possible that the process will come to an end, and you have learned more but have not succeeded and need to work through the process again, bringing to bear what you have learned.

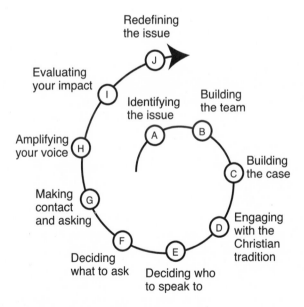

Figure 4: Justice-seeking cycle.

You may recognize the eight steps as having some similarity to the pastoral cycle, the most common method of theological reflection. The pastoral cycle is a series of four steps: description of experience, analysis, reflection in conversation with the Christian tradition, and planning leading to action. The cycle takes those who use it to a new place from which they have fresh experience upon which to build further use of the cycle.

A common criticism of the pastoral cycle by practical theologians is that theology can become 'a step in the process' and that God is 'brought in' at the reflection stage but is otherwise kept at the margins. If, as I suggested in Chapter 1, the local church becomes a fertile soil cultivating those who seek justice, then God should be present in every step.

This is also the chapter where the two case studies are introduced. The chapter will start with a segment of the case study from Coalham and end with a segment from Riverford.

Coalham case study

When Ian had told the bishop that he would serve anywhere as a curate, he hadn't really envisaged that might mean what his friends were calling 'the middle of nowhere'. Coalham was a former mining village 45 minutes by car from Scholarton, where he had gone to university and then trained for ordained Anglican ministry. His 'boss', the vicar, was responsible for five villages, each with a parish church. Ian was assigned the church in Coalham to look after, as the church still owned the vicarage. The vicar said that having his own parish was the best way to learn and that he should feel free to use his initiative. The church hall was being used to distribute food from the Scholarton food bank, and so he might want to keep an eye on that.

In the evenings when he wasn't working, Ian longed to get in the car and drive back to the comfortable social life he had enjoyed in Scholarton. He knew he must try to have some local roots, so after a few weeks he went into

---

the pub. As he feared, he was stared at as he bought his drink. Looking round, one face smiled at him. He recognized John, who stood at the back of the church after the service waiting to give his wife a lift home. He joined the circle of men sitting with John and was introduced. Gradually John drew him into the conversation. A few weeks later Ian asked, 'Why do you think the village needs a food bank?' Ian was taken aback by the heated discussion, which polarized around two views: the Job Centre in Scholarton was run by unreasonable people and young people in the village did not make enough effort to find work.

Your starting point

In this chapter, I discuss how an individual or group might discern what issue to work on and who else might be their allies in working on that issue.

You may have picked up this book with a burning question of injustice already in your mind and be looking for advice on how to take it forward. This is the road into working for justice that many people take. However, I would encourage you still to read this chapter and take time to discern what you know about this issue and why it matters to you. For others, there may be a growing awareness of injustice as a result of the social engagement of your local church or your own experience. For others, it may be realizing that you have some of the skills and spiritual dispositions described in Chapter 4, which leads you to want to make them available to those wrestling with the day-to-day reality of injustice.

If seeking after justice is to be understood as a practice of the Church rather than a personal project, it is necessary to start by drawing God into the conversation at the outset. I have called this chapter 'What is the Burning Issue?' because the sense of burning tells us that this is a desire of the human heart, a desire therefore that will already be known to God and so a desire that can be offered to him for shaping and sifting.

The starting point is the contemplation of God. The Church worships a God who has justice, righteousness and compassion in his character, and he evokes in us a desire to share in that justice, righteousness and compassion. We wonder that God is mindful of humans given their ability to despoil creation and treat each other in a way that defaces his image in them. We are humbled by the way in which God goes before any activity of ours to recognize the oppressed and overlooked. No one escapes his concern and no injustice fails to pain and anger him.

If at the point of reading this, you are on your own, wondering if action seeking justice is possible, it would be appropriate to spend some time in contemplation seeking discernment as to what your next conversation should be. If at the point of reading this you already have two or more people wanting to work together, then spending time in worship that focuses on the character of God can set the tone for what follows.

What do we know about?

Seeking justice means learning enough about an issue to know what to ask for, who to ask and when and how to ask. Our desire for justice is likely to be shaped by what we know and who we know. A good place to start in identifying an issue to work on is to review what we know about already.

What is to hand?

In the Introduction, I outlined developments in the life of the local church that I felt would raise questions of justice. I also suggested that those directly involved in new forms of practical action or relationship-building might not be the first people to ask the 'Why?' questions about situations of need or injustice. However, for those seeking justice, the work of the local church going on around us is a good place to start asking 'Why?' questions. It will mean we ask questions rooted in the communities we serve, which are real rather than hypothetical; it will mean we seek real change for identifiable people.

The social action of the local church seems the most obvious place to start in asking questions of injustice. If an issue has arisen, and the church has felt impelled to deploy resources of buildings, volunteers and money in addressing that issue, and people have come forward to benefit from that action, it is real. For those who have invested their time, energy and spiritual desires in social action projects, it can feel threatening to have someone ask, however gently, 'Why is this project needed?' That question can tend to imply, 'How can we change things so this project is no longer needed?' Although that might be accepted as a proposition, at an emotional level it can be difficult to hear. It follows from this that relationships of trust are needed between activists and reflectors, if each is to appreciate the desires of the other to participate in the character of God. God's justice does not close down his compassion.

Many churches or groups of churches are undertaking initiatives under the banner of chaplaincy (Slater 2015). This usually means that one or more church representatives have embedded themselves in a local organization or institution that values a pastoral presence. Examples include old people's homes, sports teams, shopping centres, schools and colleges, and drop-in centres, but the diversity is immense. What distinguishes chaplaincy as a form of ministry is that it is embedded in the structures of the world rather than the structures of the Church. It learns to see the world as that institution sees it, as an honorary insider. This perspective brings with it new understandings of the lives affected by that institution. Injustices that were previously invisible can become apparent. In seeking to work with these injustices it is important not to abuse the hospitality of the host organization. Again there is a relationship of trust between the chaplain and the organization that can be built on but should not be undermined.

New forms of evangelization are bringing local churches

into contact with neighbours who were formerly strangers. In attempting to enculturate the gospel within an aspect of our society, we learn that every subculture contains that which reflects the gospel and that which can subvert the gospel (Cameron 2010, Conclusions). We are also challenged to look afresh at the subculture we take for granted and see that it too contains elements that fall short of the gospel. This can provide areas for exploration and 'why questions' that had not previously occurred to us.

In many parts of the country new forms of activism have been generated ecumenically. This may include cold weather shelters, street pastor groups and food banks, but again the diversity is immense. There are also some areas where ecumenical groups study and pray together in Lent or Advent as a means of building deeper relationships in the body of Christ. Both shared activism and reflection seem to have the potential to generate 'why questions' and people with sufficient mutual trust to work on them together.

In this section, I have suggested that you start with what is to hand. This may mean listening to people who see their ministry and mission very differently from you. A work of reconciliation may be required within the life of the church before relationships can be built externally. That work will bear fruit in the integrity of the justice-seeking, which will be based upon a knowledge of reality that is relational and not just factual.

The metaphor from Paul of seeking the mind of Christ seems apt in this context. Christ is the head of the body which is his Church. The other members draw their unity from their participation in him. They also gain humility from their recognition of their interdependence and shared life.

What do we care about?

The previous section focused on what we know and the injustices that reveals to us. The reason for starting there will be discussed in the next chapter, but it is common for those interested in justice to have a spirituality that starts in the head, based on a desire to know God and understand him. This section looks at the heart and the relationships that shape our sense of ourselves and our community. This is not to suggest that those who start with the head are uncaring, but that we can start from different places and still find a point of collaboration.

Our vision of human flourishing

For some their sense of injustice comes from a keen sense of how the world should be and an anger that not all those around them are flourishing as God intended. Denominations and ecumenical and interfaith groups have put energy into expressing their vision of human flourishing as a way of highlighting where our current social arrangements fall short.

For the 2010 general election in the UK, the Catholic Bishops Conference produced a document about the Common Good (CBCEW 2008). Since then, over a dozen cities have held Fairness Commissions looking at how inequalities can be addressed. See, for example, the Sheffield Fairness Commission (2013).

An initiative in Liverpool has sought to create an ecumenical dialogue around the Common Good (see http://togetherforthe commongood.co.uk). It has taken this further, seeking to create a methodology whereby those with a different stake in social problems can come together and find ways forward.

These activities have the positive value of building institutional relationships which can be used in seeking justice and in building trust between people of goodwill. They are also significant in inspiring local churches to see that they are not on their own in taking justice seriously. There are also organizations that support local churches in their interest in justice relating to particular topics, for example Church Action on Poverty, Housing Justice, and A Rocha.

This activity and relationship-building offers a framework for the local church. However, it is also important to start with the relationships that matter to us now in this community. Some of those will be the same as those outlined in the previous section. But there may be others that arise from the work or ministry of church members, for example the local school or old people's home or charities or community groups. These relationships create a sense of participation in the injustices of others and the beginnings of trust that will allow justice-seeking to take place.

Here the metaphor of our hearts burning within us taken from the story of the road to Emmaus suggests that relationships can be punctuated with moments of recognition when we realize that the Spirit is at work.

Who else is concerned?

Having gone through a process of discernment that engages mind and heart, it should be possible to identify one or more issues that could be worked with. Either as part of the process of reaching certainty or as a next step in the process, it is helpful to undertake a stakeholder analysis. Another task at this point is to identify local agencies who may be able to support those we may come across in the justice-seeking journey.

Stakeholder analysis

Stakeholder analysis is a tool from management studies that helps a group of people analyse who they think has an interest (or stake) in the topic that is of concern to them. The exercise can be undertaken by drawing a diagram and so can be a good way of creating participation when a group first starts to work together.

The issue is written in a circle in the middle of a large piece of paper. People take it in turns to call out other individuals, groups or organizations who they think have an interest in the topic or a stake in what happens. Each suggestion is written down round the edge of the page with a line linking it to the topic in the middle.

The second stage is to get a second sheet of paper and again put the issue in the middle of the page. This time, for each of the suggestions made on the first page a decision is made whether to write it on the top half of the page as a potential ally or on the bottom half as someone where their position is unknown or where there might be resistance to change. Either at the same time or as a third stage an attempt is made to vary the length of the line linking the name to the circle. This indicates the strength of the connection to the issue. Is this of central concern or peripheral to the stakeholder? Is there a strong ability to influence the outcome or a weak one?

The final stage is to identify where relationships already exist and who has them, and then to underline where relationships would be helpful and decide who is best placed to build them. If a stakeholder has been identified who may have to be asked to change what they do, it is probably better to find out what can be known without actually contacting them at this stage. The rationale for this will become apparent in Chapter 7.

Knowing who can help when you can't

In the process of building relationships it is likely that people will be encountered who express needs which it is beyond the scope of the group or local churches to meet. It is important to have a map of local agencies that are able to offer advice and support and to know how to refer to them. Ideally personal relationships will be built so that referral is a personal rather than impersonal transaction. It may well be that someone within the local churches has already come up with such a map and that they are willing for you to adapt it for your own purposes.

Riverford case study

Jane had mixed feelings about coffee after Sunday morning worship. As a solicitor she often found herself being asked for free advice. In fact, at least once a month she and her husband tried to escape to their holiday cottage a couple of hours away. They had moved from London to Holtbridge for all the right reasons when the children were small, but it had put severe limitations on her career, and now the boys were at university she increasingly felt the need to escape. Irene ran Messy Church, a family-friendly session involving craft activities, food and Bible stories. Irene said she needed to talk to Jane about one of the Messy Church mums. Jane braced herself for an advice session. It was a complicated story of divorce, bankruptcy and an unpaid mortgage. The mother and children were now living in emergency accommodation in the large village of River-ford, and the teenage girl was getting the bus into the secondary school in Holtbridge. There was nowhere for her to do her homework, and her mother was frantic that this would affect her exam results. Irene said she was appeal-ing to Jane as a governor of the Holtbridge Academy to do something. Jane said something about looking into it but had no real idea about what that might mean.

A couple of days later Jane phoned up the deputy head, Mr Owen, saying she had a Riverford parent who was concerned about homework facilities and wondered what the situation was. Mr Owen explained that the Riverford children left as soon as the school day finished on a bus that took them back home. They only did after-school activities, such as the homework club, if they had parents who could pick them up. This was just the reality of a large academy serving a town and several satellite villages. The word 'reality' irked Jane; she would not have accepted it if it had been applied to her boys. She asked if she could come in and meet the Year 11 students who came from Riverford. Rather surprised, the deputy head said he would see what he could do.

4

Building the Team

Coalham case study

At the end of the service, Ian spotted John who smiled at him and said, 'Well you certainly got them talking!' Ian said he was already talking to Keith, who ran the food bank. 'You should speak to Leanne at the school,' John advised. 'There is not much happening in this village that gets past her.'

Ian learned from Keith that, from the vouchers that people presented when they collected their food parcels, 40 per cent of people were saying they needed emergency food because their benefits had been sanctioned. Leanne, the school family liaison officer, said that when parents asked her for food bank vouchers, it was often because their benefits had been stopped. She felt it needed looking into because the food parcels lasted a week and some people were getting their benefits stopped for a couple of months. The parting words of his college tutor now made sense to Ian – 'Don't start anything that depends on you, you're only there for three years.' Ian went back to John and asked if he would lead a team to look into things. He had been impressed by the gentle way in which John had included him in his circle of friends at the pub and the heated but friendly way in which they had disagreed with each other. John advised that they would definitely need someone who was good with computers, everything did these days. He volunteered his nephew Mark who had finished FE college but still not got a job. Keith suggested Nick and Oona, who both worked in Scholarton and attended the Roman Catholic church there and helped him by running food parcels between the two places. Oona was a ward clerk in the hospital and willing to help the group stay organized. Nick was an inspector on the buses supervising drivers and a member of the parish Justice and Peace Group.

The team met in Ian's front room. John started by asking if they agreed that what was bringing them together was the question of why people in Coalham were having their benefits sanctioned. Mark went red, he hadn't told his parents but he had had his benefits stopped for failing to turn up at the Job Centre. He felt he had experience as well as skills to offer.

If justice-seeking is a practice of the local church, then it is most faithful to our understanding of the body of Christ if it is undertaken by a group of people. It is possible to bring about change as a lone citizen, and it may well be that an individual seeks the support of their church in taking on an issue of personal concern to them. The purpose of this chapter is to show how working as a team can enrich justice-seeking for all concerned.

As the previous chapter described, the 'why questions' that become the starting point for justice-seeking can be triggered in a number of ways. The question may suggest the sources from which a team can be drawn. If a street pastors group has been set up ecumenically and gets drawn into issues of rough sleeping, then it may be logical to go to the churches that supply the street pastors and ask if they have members who would like to work on the provision of direct-access beds for rough sleepers. If a city-centre church has sponsored a town-centre chaplaincy and become aware of the high number of shop staff on zero-hours contracts, then a group may come together in that church to challenge that practice. A group of churches running a food bank may not have the capacity to challenge the injustices they are aware of but they could appeal to the churches and schools that are donating food for people, who might want to form a 'justice group' to support them.

Recruiting the right skills

Most groups start with a nucleus of people who already know each other or an individual who persuades a few people that they want to meet. The early meetings of this nucleus are important for building trusting relationships and identifying who else might be drawn into the group, then seeking them out and giving them time to reflect and respond.

There are some skills that it might be helpful to include in the group. There are often people who bring more than one thing to a group so the size of the group is not determined by this list of skills.

A facilitator is important to the effective working of group meetings. They can ensure that all group members' contributions are drawn into the discussion and that the group both defines and sticks to its task. They need not be knowledgeable about the issue; in fact a lack of knowledge can help ensure that all group members play their part. To facilitate is not the same as being good at chairing meetings. A good chair has many similar skills but will be focused on making decisions and getting through the agenda in a timely manner. A facilitator will give the group permission to explore new angles that come up and will ensure that decisions are taken by the group. The facilitator can also monitor the energy levels in the group and help it reflect upon how the work is going (J. Rogers 2010; Widdicombe 2000). Every member of the team will need to be willing to listen to each other, but it will be helpful if at least one person is able to go and talk to people who are affected by or involved in the issue. An ability to listen to people on their own terms without imposing an agenda is crucial, if the change that is asked for is to be appropriate for the people affected.

An important skill is that of research. A surprising amount can be found out via the internet and by sending emails. It needs to be done in a thorough and methodical way and the information found recorded in a way that is accessible to the group. If research is about finding the right information, then networking is about finding the right people. An ability to pick up the phone or just buttonhole someone and ask directly for a link to another person is vital.

A crucial part of the process is asking for change. That asking is likely to be done in writing or in a verbal presentation. The team needs someone who can do that or who can check that written and verbal presentations are well expressed with good spelling and grammar. Many organizations judge the content of a request by the quality of the communication.

Every team needs someone who keeps accurate records of their meetings, ensures the information they have gathered is securely stored and arranges the dates and venues for meetings.

The group will also benefit from someone with a good know-ledge of the Christian tradition when they come to discuss the gap between how things are and how they would wish them to be. That is a moral discussion and so someone with experience of theological reflection will be an asset. This may be a role that someone training for ministry can take on.

Teams can often function adequately with a missing skill when the facilitator reminds the group that that skill is not around the table, and so they must find ways of compensating for it between them.

Discerning spiritual gifts and temptations

The language of skill used in the previous section can suggest that justice-seeking is a rational process that is somehow sepa-rate from the spiritual. This would be to cut across the idea of integrated mission this book advocates. An equally important part of building a team is to think about the spiritual gifts and dispositions members bring.

A way of thinking about this that I have found helpful is drawn from the Enneagram, a model of thinking about spirituality used in both Christian and secular settings. There is a substantial body of knowledge and wisdom here that can be used by individuals and groups to reflect upon their dispositions to build on their strengths and avoid being trapped by their temptations to stay rigidly within those strengths. It also gives insights into how people with different dispositions might effectively work together (Riso and Hudson 1999; Palmer 1995).

In this chapter I want to take one insight from the Enneagram and use it as a starting point for a team wanting to seek justice. The insight is that people tend to have a dominant source for their spirituality that shapes their way of relating to God. The three sources are head, heart and hand. Those whose spirituality starts with the head seek to understand God both as he has revealed himself and in his mystery. Those whose spirituality starts with the heart seek to be in relationship with God. Those whose spirituality starts with the hand seek to serve God. The Enneagram suggests that while for all of us there will be a mixture of knowing, relating and doing, we will have a starting point.

My own speculation is that these preferences have shaped the culture of some local churches and even some denominations. In my own denomination, the metaphor of service is found in clothing, the design of buildings, the wording of important ceremonies and many other ways. The metaphors of knowing and relating are also there but not as prominent (Shakespeare 2014). Spending time in a Quaker retreat house I realized that learning about God and the ways in which he might be understood and what might be learned from other Friends was an important metaphor. The Bible and the book of *Quaker Faith and Practice* were on the table around which we gathered for worship.

It seems likely that people who have the tenacity to pursue the 'why questions' that seek justice will have a spirituality that starts from the head. Those with a hand spirituality will wish to prioritize the service of those experiencing the injustice. Those with a heart spirituality will want to build relationships that link them with those who might help them. In seeking justice it is the first-hand knowledge of the person who serves that may raise the issue, and the bridge-building skills of the person who relates that builds the relationships that may address the issue, but it will be the desire to understand the situation from the person who starts from the head that is likely to sustain the momentum.

Paul's metaphor of the body of Christ shows that all are needed and that our aim should be interdependence. However, given our human frailty it is unsurprising that we should find it difficult to sustain mutual sympathy when we start in different places. So, to spell out what this might mean in a local church community, it may well be that the activists and relators need to make room for the more reflective head spirituality. Impatience at what may seem like passivity may have to be overcome to benefit from the enquiring mind and tenacity that justice-seeking requires. This may even be true at the ecumenical level – churches that produce a lot of activists may have to turn to churches of different traditions to help form a team that will be effective in justice-seeking.

However, if the team is all head, it will lack the capacity to build trusting relationships with those who have the power to change things. If the team excludes activists or at least fails to listen to them regularly, then there is a danger that their work will drift away from the real issue and lose any sense of momentum.

The Enneagram also suggests that alongside the dispositions of head, heart and hand go 'temptations' or dominant reactions to adversity. Hand people tend to react most commonly with anger. That is positive in that it creates the energy to bring about change, but it can also lead to despair that any changes to systems and structures are possible and that the only way forward is to help individuals one at a time. Heart people tend to react with fear. The positive aspect of this is that it can indicate where power relations lie and what the source of

oppression is. It can, however, immobilize and make it difficult to challenge people in power and make them feel that the
only way forward is to comfort the afflicted. Head people can
experience shame that the world is unjust, and while that can
generate a desire to understand it can also create a sense of
unworthiness and an anxiety about the Church speaking out.
They can feel that the Church has to be reformed before the
systems and structures of the world can be challenged.

Being part of a justice-seeking group can help build self-
awareness about these spiritual starting points and the benefits
and limitations that go with them. It also has the potential
for gentle mutual appreciation and correction, reflecting back
things that group members are saying for further consideration.

Speaking about the team at this level of spiritual interdependence raises the question of whether people of other
faiths or none can be drawn in. This is clearly a matter for local
discernment. My own position would be that justice-seeking
is a moral task and that that moral element needs to be both
acknowledged and open to discussion. If all the group members
are willing to engage in moral debate, then a basis for acting
together should develop. It is possible to do this type of work
in a pragmatic, problem-solving way that looks for what works
and ignores moral questions. For me, fundamental to seeking
justice is knowing why what you ask for is less oppressive or
unjust than the current situation. It is possible for people of
goodwill to disagree about which solution is better and so
there needs to be some criteria for evaluating ways forward.
An example would be that it is often possible to improve the
resources available to provide a service, if the terms and conditions of employment of those who deliver the service are
made less generous. It is then necessary to balance the needs of
those providing the service against the needs of those receiving
it. That is a moral rather than a pragmatic question.

Chapter 6 will discuss how the moral aspect of seeking justice can be tackled by engaging with the Christian tradition.
My belief is that this is a public tradition which all citizens can
engage with as part of their moral reflections. I do realize there

are contexts in which that might be seen as a dominating move by Christians and so a different range of resources may need to be drawn upon for moral reflection.

Agreeing ways of working together

Strong teams are able to talk about how they can best work together. Where a team is drawn from members of the same local church or denomination there is the possibility that they adopt the conventions of a church committee meeting that they are familiar with. That may work well but it may be either too hierarchical or too open ended for this task. It is good to agree on some parameters for the group that can be revisited if necessary. How often will the group meet (start and end times and venue)? Is everyone able to participate on an equal basis or do some people need financial or practical support with travel and child care? To whom does the group regard itself as accountable? Is it all right to interrupt one another and, if not, how does a member signal that they want to make a point?

Although church groups are often quite informal, it can be helpful to record the answers to these questions so that every group member feels empowered to raise them again if they have concerns about the group's effectiveness or their ability to participate.

Beyond these practicalities of working together is the important issue of how the group will make decisions. Discernment is again a spiritual gift and a group of people can learn to use that gift together. Some will have a particular denominational tradition they can offer; others will wish to take time to pray when important decisions are being made. Some will be happy with a voting majority; others will feel uncomfortable if a consensus is not reached. Identifying early important decisions and then reflecting upon how they were reached will help the team build up its approach to decision-making and discernment.

Identifying partners

At the point at which the group has formed, it is helpful to repeat the stakeholder exercise described at the end of the previous chapter. It will enable the person who first raised the justice issue to clarify what the concern is and how they understand it fitting into existing systems and structures. With the benefit of the wider perspective the group brings it is possible to think about who might be able to help with the issue to be tackled.

Are there other churches and voluntary agencies providing a service that is relevant to the issue and, if so, what are their perspectives on it? Do local advice agencies have other people bringing this issue to them and, if so, do they know how many, and have they sought to challenge the injustice? Looking at the websites of local politicians and Members of Parliament, does it look as if any of them have taken an interest in this issue? Does an internet search or shared knowledge reveal any campaigning organizations, trade unions or academics that might have already done research?

Making contact with potential partners and evaluating what you learn is an important step in understanding the landscape within which you will be operating.

Some potential partners may wish to co-opt your efforts to theirs. This can be a good and quick way forward. But it is also worth thinking about whether your group has a distinctive agenda or focus that might get lost by partnering at this early stage. There may be a county campaign about the closure of libraries, but if you are concerned with the delivery of library books to older and disabled people in your village, then might your concerns get lost in the wider campaign? A local advice agency might have made representations to a private landlord offering substandard accommodation but it may be that the examples you bring might have a different impact. These again are matters of discernment and so the group will need to draw upon its shared practices.

Riverford case study

Jane walked from her office to the Holtbridge Academy. Mr Owen had managed to assemble four students willing to talk to her at the end of the lunch break – Lee, Michelle, Niamh and Pete, who turned out to be Lee's older brother and in the sixth form. Jane explained that as a governor she was interested in all students in the school having the same chance of success. She understood that students from Riverford missed out on after-school activities. Pete acted as spokesman. 'The bus leaves as soon as school is over, and we have to go home with our younger brothers and sisters to make sure everything is okay back at home before our parents get home from work. There are loads more things to do at school and in Holtbridge but basically nothing in Riverford.' Niamh said that she was sharing a bedroom with her little sister, and so there was nowhere she could do her homework.

Jane asked if she could write to their parents and ask if they could meet in Riverford to look at whether there were any solutions to the problem. She was encouraged by their enthusiasm.

Mr Owen said he'd mention all this to the headteacher. It wasn't the normal sort of thing governors got involved in, but if a group of students wanted to do it as a citizenship project it would probably be okay. She would need someone to work with her in Riverford, so she was not alone with the students. He also helpfully added that the Academy had some funding to extend the school day but that naturally it wanted to invest that money in facilities at the school.

As she walked back to her office Jane knew exactly who she needed to get on board. The chapel in Riverford only had one service a month now, but the Steward, Mrs Kaye, was determined to keep the doors open. She would let them use the chapel to meet in and give Jane some moral support.

5

Building the Case for Change

Coalham case study

Keith and Leanne found five people they knew who were willing to talk about their benefits being sanctioned. John and Nick agreed they would meet with them in either the pub or the church hall and find out what they thought the problem was and what they wanted to be done. The main problem seemed to be sanctions imposed because they had failed to turn up to a meeting either at the Job Centre or with the Work Programme office. This was because the appointments were either too early for the first bus from Coalham, or because they couldn't afford to get the bus in more than one day a week. Four of the five agreed that John and Nick could stay in touch and ask further questions. They were happy for the team to see what could be done, although pretty sure that nothing was possible, it was just the system.

Oona said that in her years of working for the NHS she'd never met an unreasonable person who didn't think they had a reason for their actions, and so she would go and talk to the staff at the Job Centre and the Work Programme office. She reported back that she had got nowhere with the Job Centre. They wouldn't talk to her, because she wasn't a claimant or directly representing a claimant. Her meeting at the Work Programme office went much better. The manager said that he would email clients from Coalham

---

and say they could ask to change the day of their appointment if the Job Centre asked them to come in on a different day. He would also remind them that he could refund bus fares if they were coming in for a course or a job interview. Mark had found some government statistics about the numbers of people being sanctioned. He'd also found some food bank statistics about reasons for asking for a food parcel that made it seem as if sanctions were a bigger issue for their village than other places. It looked as if they needed to persuade the Job Centre that only one visit a week was reasonable for people travelling in from Coalham.

Nick asked for permission to give feedback on their progress to the Justice and Peace Group in his parish in Scholarton. He was sure they would want to pray for the team and those affected by the problem.

This chapter deals with the investigative part of the process where listening and research skills are to the fore. The aim is to identify the change that will address the injustice and build a case that can be made to the person or body with the authority to make the change. This relies on learning about two things: the nature of the problem, and finding out how the structure or system is intended to work. The key questions are: why is this happening, how are things supposed to work and what is the case for change?

The spiritual dispositions needed in this chapter are listening, reflection and discernment. The team need to find ways of being silent for reflection and discernment as well as ways of challenging each other that are respectful but don't sweep aside some of the real ethical challenges found in this part of the process. But the chapter starts where any search for justice needs to start, by listening to the people affected by the injustice.

What do the people affected want to happen?

A starting point for justice-seeking must be to understand how the people affected by the injustice understand the situation and what they would want to happen.

This takes us back to Chapter 2, where I discussed the range of relationships that could exist between the team and the people affected by the injustice. These were: inform, support, advise, advocate with/for individuals, lobby and campaign.

It is vital that the team identify what their relationship is to the individual or group of people affected. It is always preferable to support people in advocating for themselves rather than take the matter out of their hands. However, there will be situations where a change is desired and there may be negative consequences for an individual speaking out, or they may actively wish for the issue to be taken up on their behalf, or they may have more pressing issues with survival that deflect them from advocating on their own behalf. The relationship between those affected and the team is a power relationship and both sides must be satisfied that the power is bounded, consensual and ethical.

Arriving at that relationship requires listening to people on their own terms and trying to set aside any preliminary views of the situation you may have reached. It will be necessary to take notes, and this should also be agreed with the person or people concerned so they understand what will happen to the information and views they share.

If they wish their story to be shared but their name to be withheld, it is important to check that you have sufficiently anonymized their case for them to feel they can't be recognized. If they wish to present their case in person or to be named, it is important to make sure they understand any adverse consequences that may follow from this, such as sanctioning of their benefits. Discussing possible implications for other members of their household may also affect the decisions people make about anonymity.

If the injustice involves an individual or group who have a reduced capacity to make decisions in their own best interests, then it is necessary to find someone to act as their advocate so that in the team's eagerness to tackle injustice the views and needs of those affected don't get lost.

We live in an age when people expect a photograph or video clip to be used to illustrate every point. The same level of ethical thought and care is needed in using images. It is also common to use the internet to share information. Thought needs to be given to how that information may be passed on and how it might be changed or reinterpreted in that process.

Once the team feel they have an understanding of the way in which those affected see the situation, what they would like to change and any ethical restrictions around using their story, data or image, it is helpful to produce a simple written statement of the injustice. The statement will help the team retain its focus and build a case that is relevant. Now the team is ready to start building the case.

Primary data – numbers and stories

Making a case for change starts with building a description of who is affected, how they are affected and what they would like to see happen.

Who is affected? Finding out how many people are affected can be as straightforward as counting the number of people who have come forward, or it can require some research to find out the potential size of the group affected. If a group of people are raising problems about a private landlord, is it about one particular company or is it about the agent that acts on behalf of a number of landlords? Does it affect all tenants in a particular area or does it affect a particular type of tenant? The size of a problem will often affect the way in which the people with the authority to make the change respond. If it is a single case with no repercussions, an exception might be made for an individual. If it is likely to affect a sizable number of people, there will be a need to investigate the cost and other implications of making a change. Finding out who is affected at an early stage can be helpful in deciding what to ask for first.

How are they affected? Having stories of how people have been affected is important in illustrating the problem and showing why action is necessary. However, it is important to choose stories that are representative of what you have heard and not just present the case of the person most adversely affected. If it is possible to identify categories of problem or people affected, that can help build the case. If this information is not readily to hand, it may be necessary to consider gathering data directly by knocking on doors or standing in the street with a short questionnaire (Gillham 2008).

Reflecting on what is learned from this exercise is important in ensuring a growing clarity of understanding while retaining a focus upon what needs changing. If it is unclear to the team, it will be harder to decide what to ask for.

It may become apparent that the issue is the result of the interaction between two or more agencies, systems or structures and so a wider set of information is needed than at first thought. It is often the case that recurrent problems have this inter-agency character. It may be that there are insufficient resources for the agencies to cooperate together effectively or that each perceives the problem to be the responsibility of the other. Another frequent possibility is that different levels of the organization are sending out different messages. Senior people may be suggesting that the problem can easily be resolved whereas at the front-line level there are issues that are not understood at the senior level, or resolving the issue would mean a loss of face or discretion to run things in the most convenient way.

The work needed to resolve these inter-organizational problems is called boundary-spanning. It requires exploration of what discretion each organization has and on what basis they might be willing to cooperate. It is also necessary to identify what form of ongoing connection between them is needed to prevent the problem recurring. It could be sharing information, appointing two people to undertake liaison or, at its most extreme, setting up a committee or team to work in a coordinated way.

Secondary data: comparisons and context

An important aspect of building the case for change is to put the issue into context. Most often that will mean a geographical context, but it can be context relating to how other agencies are dealing with the same group of people. Are there characteristics of the locality that affect the problem, such as a remote location, the availability of public transport, the mismatch between needs and resources in a key local agency?

The Office of National Statistics provides a wide range of data that enables you to work out whether a particular group of people are over- or under-represented in the area you are interested in. The local authority may already publish data that sets the context for the issue. The Library Service may be able to advise.

A helpful way of making the case for change can be to provide comparisons. If there are other parts of the country where the injustice you are tackling has been resolved, then you can point to those solutions as being worth considering in your locality. This is where networking with stakeholders can lead to valuable contacts to follow up. If one of your stakeholder agencies is affiliated to a national network, it may be possible to get them to ask if there are other parts of the country sharing your problem or where solutions have been found that could be offered in your locality.

Given the wide range of think tanks and academics in the UK it may well be that someone has already looked at the issue you are considering or perhaps placed it in a wider context. Now that think tanks and academics make so much of their work freely available on the internet, it is often possible to find someone who can offer some expert input. People are usually delighted when they get an email or phone call following up something they have written. Of course, think tanks and academics also have agendas, and it is important to stick to your purposes and not be co-opted into their agendas.

Freedom of Information Requests

Where information is not in the public domain and is held by a public body, it is possible to issue a Freedom of Information Request. The website 'What do they know' helps you do this and gives examples of successful requests.

Knowledge of how things should work

When a system or structure has been identified that seems to be contributing to the injustice, it is important to discover how it is intended to work. This is not as straightforward as it seems. It is not uncommon for different people to give different accounts of how things are supposed to work. This problem was set out in 1980 by an American academic called Michael Lipsky in a book called *Street-Level Bureaucrats*. He showed that there can be gaps between what politicians intend, what civil servants design and then what the agencies engaged to deliver a service to citizens actually deliver. These gaps may be due to a number of reasons. There may be insufficient resources to deliver all the aspects of the policy and so it does not meet its potential. The civil servants who commission the service may make it insufficiently clear what should be delivered and how much discretion the agency has. The agency may adopt working practices that make it more convenient or cost-effective for them to deliver the service but that subvert its original intentions. The agency may become fixated on targets, especially if some of the funding is linked to payment by results, and so lose sight of the genuine differences in need between the citizens making use of the service. The training given to the employees of the agency may not give them a clear sense of what discretion they have and how it can be used. It is cheaper for an organization to deliver a standardized service, and so there can be reluctance to make appropriate use of the discretion available.

If there is no publicly available document saying how things should work and what discretion is possible, it can be helpful to create a flow chart setting out the team's understanding of what should happen. This can be used as part of the 'asking' to check that there is a shared understanding of what is possible.

Faulty implementation versus faulty system

Once the information in this chapter has been gathered, it should become evident whether the injustice is as a result of faulty implementation of something that if it was working properly would resolve the problem, or whether the system itself is designed in a way that is producing unjust outcomes for some or all of the people using it.

Making this distinction gives a stronger basis for asking the person with the authority to change things to do so. If it is a problem of implementation, then the team are in a strong position to ask for things to be put right in a timely manner, even if it costs the agency more or means it will have to change the way it does things.

If the system needs changing, then a more thorough case for why this should be done, and a thorough analysis of who has the authority to change the system, needs to be undertaken.

In practice, if the information about how things should work proves difficult to uncover, it can be good to start by assuming that it is a problem of faulty implementation and then learning from the response to the request for redress the ways in which you might be dealing with a faulty system. At the point at which you have an understanding about the gap between how things are and how they should be, it is important to return to those affected by the injustice and ask how they would like to see the gap dealt with. If the team is acting as agents on behalf of a specific person or group of people, it will be important to continue to act as a go-between.

This is a good moment to revisit the stakeholder analysis undertaken at the end of Chapter 3. Has your understanding of the role and relative power of the different stakeholders changed as a result of what you have learned? It is also important at the conclusion of this stage to look again at the statement of what you think the issue is, how you think things should be working, and the gap to be addressed. Updating this shared document will help the team retain its focus as it works through the next three chapters.

Riverford case study

Not only had Mrs Kaye opened the chapel in Riverford, she'd put the kettle on and bought some chocolate biscuits. To Jane's surprise, Lee, Michelle and Pete already knew Mrs Kaye and were bringing her up to date on their families. Until five years ago, Mrs Kaye had run holiday clubs in the chapel at half-terms. Jane asked what had brought them to an end, and Mrs Kaye said that she had run out of energy and volunteers.

The students said that they would like the school to look at running a second bus, so they could choose when to come home, or they would like somewhere they could go in Riverford that had computers and internet. The obvious place was the library, but that now closed at 3.30 p.m., as they got off the bus. Mrs Kaye confirmed that the local authority cuts meant that the library was open fewer hours. If they were going to make a case for change to the Academy, then they would need to know what other students thought. They came up with a survey that they could give out on the bus. Pete said he would ask Mr Owen for permission. Niamh and Michelle said they would make sure all the Year 10 and 11 students filled it in. Mrs Kaye offered to go into the library and find out more about their facilities and why their hours were reduced.

The survey showed that three-quarters of the students were in favour of somewhere in Riverford to go to do homework at evenings and weekends. They all knew each other from the primary school in Riverford and wanted to have their own space.

Jane knew from her years as a school governor that what shifted the mind of the governing body was information about student attainment. With the group's permission she asked Mr Owen if the school office could produce anonymous data on the GCSE results for Riverford students compared to the school as a whole. There wasn't a huge difference, but it was statistically significant, and it was there for every year group. There was no means of linking it to homework facilities, but it put the discussion in a different light.

6

Engaging with the Christian Tradition

Coalham case study

If they were going to ask for change, they needed to know that what they were asking for was not only reasonable but the right thing. Ian had done theological reflection at college, but there with his fellow students it had seemed a good way to challenge each other's assumptions. In this context it felt more real. Ian decided to use a thematic approach and got the group to discuss three themes that summed up the liberation message of the New Testament. After discussion, they were able to agree on three things:

- People in Coalham needed to have hope and that any positive change could help bring hope.
- Coalham was a marginalized community and deserved additional help to put it on the same basis as Scholarton.
- Ensuring the Job Centre understood the problems they were causing and being prepared to take it further if necessary was part of 'telling it as it is'.

On what basis is this change being sought?

By this stage in the process the team should have an understanding of the injustice they are tackling, some idea of how things should work and what change they might need to ask for. If the dialogue with those directly affected by the issue has been maintained, then there will be some knowledge of how they would like to see the situation resolved.

To stop at this point and attempt to listen to the voice of the Christian tradition may feel either artificial or unnecessary. A significant amount of Christian action takes place under-pinned by prayer and worship, but not specifically seeking to make reference to the Christian tradition. What is more, what is understood to be the Christian tradition varies between Christians. All would see the Bible as important, but many would also see historic writings from their own strand of Christianity as an equally important guide. Some might feel that the Bible was not an appropriate document to use in discussing public matters when not all those affected would subscribe to its importance. Others might feel that only experts aware of the historic background of the Bible can interpret it. Others might wonder whether they would be taken seriously if their moral reasoning was based upon a book that is seen as being for the private use of Christians and in worship (Cameron et al. 2012, Chapter 6).

I personally favour using the Bible, because it has withstood the disagreements that Christians have had about it, and it has a history in the UK of being a public document which people can discuss and debate. In a post-secular society, people of faith cannot pretend that their world view comes from a list of values; they need to be open about the fact that a body of tradition and scripture is given a level of authority by them in the process of making moral decisions. To name something as unjust and to ask for action to remedy it is to make a moral argument, and making the basis of that argument transparent enables others to challenge the moral basis of their position.

In Chapter 4 I discussed building the team and suggested that the team would need to agree that they would discuss the moral and ethical aspects of their work. The team has come together to seek justice as an outworking of their Christian identity, no matter how tentative or emergent that identity is. They are not seeking to win awards for theological sophistication or to pass exams. Each member will have something to bring to the discussion and an ability to ask questions of the others. If discernment is seen as a gift of the Spirit to be received, rather than an intellectual achievement to be grasped, then the group will work in a way that meets its purposes. It is also important to say that this is a way of working that comes with practice and that each practice develops from a first attempt.

Approach 1: Listening for resonances

As the group discusses the change they seek, they can listen for resonances in that part of the Christian tradition to which they have access. It may be a remembered quotation, a line from a hymn, a passage of scripture. It may involve searching on key words or phrases. There is often more of the Christian tradition embedded in our memories than we realize, and conversation can draw out resonances. Some people are adept at using online reference tools. There may also be someone in the team who is theologically educated and so is able to guide the group to parts of the tradition that are worth considering. I find biblical stories particularly helpful in giving people space to offer a range of interpretations and for new insights to be sparked off in the conversation. The book *Resourcing Mission* contains a number of examples of this approach (Cameron 2010), linked to case studies of local churches.

Approach 2: A thematic approach

Another approach that can help overcome anxieties about lack of expertise is to take a thematic approach and use a major theme or themes from the Bible to challenge the team's thinking. This was the approach I took with colleagues in the book *Theological Reflection for Human Flourishing*. Professor Christopher Rowland developed three themes that summarized the liberative message of the New Testament and that were included in Chapter 5 of the book. He has given permission for me to reproduce them here. I have since used them with other groups and found them a powerful means of generating new insights into issues.

Taking your reflections forward

Being able to articulate the moral basis for the request will enable the team to accept and reflect upon the responses they receive when they ask for change. If they are offered compromises rather than exactly what they ask, it should help them decide whether they wish to accept them.

The rest of this chapter sets out the three themes adapted from *Theological Reflection for Human Flourishing* (Cameron et al. 2012):

Theme A: The breaking in of the kingdom

With the coming of Christ a new age has decisively broken in. We are invited to experience life in all its fullness. We are called to act as if it is already real while being aware that it is not yet fully realized. This enables us to hold hope and reality in tension.

Jesus' sermon at the synagogue in Nazareth sees him announcing the year of the Lord, a decisive turn in history.

> He stood up to read, and the scroll of the prophet Isaiah was given to him. He unrolled the scroll and found the place where it was written:
> 'The Spirit of the Lord is upon me,
>   because he has anointed me
>   to bring good news to the poor.
> He has sent me to proclaim release to the captives
>   and recovery of sight to the blind,
>   to let the oppressed go free,
> to proclaim the year of the Lord's favour.'

And he rolled up the scroll, gave it back to the attendant, and sat down. The eyes of all in the synagogue were fixed on him. Then he began to say to them, 'Today this scripture has been fulfilled in your hearing.' (Luke 4.16–21)

Central to the Christian hope for human flourishing is the struggle to taste heaven on earth. This is exemplified in the Lord's Prayer:

> 'Pray then in this way:
> Our Father in heaven,
>   hallowed be your name.
>   Your kingdom come.
>   Your will be done,
>   on earth as it is in heaven.
>   Give us this day our daily bread.
>   And forgive us our debts,
>   as we also have forgiven our debtors.
>   And do not bring us to the time of trial,
>   but rescue us from the evil one.' (Matt. 6.9–13)

The priorities of the kingdom of heaven turn out to be different from what people are expecting. Justice seems to be related to needs rather than deserts, and status comes through service rather than position. Matthew 20 contains two illustrative stories. The first (Matt. 20.1–16) is a parable in which a landowner hires day labourers to work in his vineyard at an agreed daily rate. He returns to the market and recruits further labourers during the course of the day. At the end of the day he pays each person the same amount. Those who have 'borne the burden of the day and the scorching heat' complain that they have been badly treated. The employer asserts his right to be generous. The parable concludes, 'So the last will be first, and the first will be last' (Matt. 20.16).

The second is an account of a conversation between Jesus and the mother of two of his disciples. In response to Mrs Zebedee's request that her sons sit at the right and left hand of Jesus when he comes into his kingdom, Jesus reasserts the priorities of the kingdom:

> 'You know that the rulers of the Gentiles lord it over them, and their great ones are tyrants over them. It will not be so among you; but whoever wishes to be great among you must be your servant, and whoever wishes to be first among you must be your slave; just as the Son of Man came not to be served but to serve, and to give his life a ransom for many.' (Matt. 20.25–28)

The confidence to enact the kingdom while accepting that all is not as we would wish is central to Christian hope. The kingdom is already inaugurated by Christ's life, death and resurrection but it is yet to be fully realized. Wheat and weeds continue to grow together (Matt. 13.24–30).

Theme B: Christ's love crosses boundaries

Those on the edge are now in the centre: for example, the child, the untouchable leper, and the possessed. The Church exemplifies a community of equals in which our differences are a source of strength, albeit problematic at times. The governing principle is love.

The Gospels are full of stories that show Christ crossing boundaries of social acceptability. These stories have given Christians a special concern for the marginalized.

Jesus presents the child as an exemplar of the kingdom: 'Whoever becomes humble like this child is the greatest in the kingdom of heaven. Whoever welcomes one such child in my name welcomes me' (Matt. 18.4–5).

In the story of the Canaanite woman (Matt. 15.21–26) Jesus suggests to the woman that his ministry is only to the house of Israel. She replies, 'Yes, Lord, yet even the dogs eat the crumbs that fall from their masters' table' (v. 27). By acknowledging her excluded status as a non-Jew, the woman pushes for inclusion in the banquet of the kingdom. Jesus commends her and grants her request.

In all our societies there remain boundaries to be crossed.

> A leper came to him begging him, and kneeling he said to him, 'If you choose, you can make me clean.' Moved with pity, Jesus stretched out his hand and touched him, and said to him, 'I do choose. Be made clean!' (Mark 1.40–41)

In these gospel passages we can see a struggle to bring what is marginalized to the centre of attention.

Paul helps the Corinthians understand their incorporation into Christ and so their responsibility as members (see 1 Cor. 12 and 13). He urges them to overcome their divisions by seeing love as the power that unifies and animates the body. He acknowledges the limitations of our current knowledge of God but promises a fulfilment of God's love.

> For now we see in a mirror, dimly, but then we will see face to face. Now I know only in part; then I will know fully, even as I have been fully known. And now faith, hope, and love abide, these three; and the greatest of these is love. (1 Cor. 13.12–13)

Bringing the language of love to the situations we encounter is a constant struggle when the world offers us languages of power and control.

Theme C: Unmasking the empire

The principalities and powers, economic and political, can be unmasked for what they are. They may hold sway now but in the end evil will be defeated. A key is naming that which is antagonistic to human flourishing. In a desire to get the best out of the system for those we are seeking to help, it is tempting not to name the political and economic realities we encounter.

The strand of apocalyptic literature in the Bible uses highly symbolic language to do that naming. It is as if the imagery sets the writers free to tell it as it is. They describe vividly that which seeks to overcome good and long for its downfall. The writer of Revelation is thought to have been wrestling with the evils of the Roman Empire, whose power seemed so total and unassailable. Some of us live in situations of political terror or totalitarianism. For others this is a time of shifting foundations when people struggle to name what is good and what is bad in the systems that shape their lives. The misuse of power by media, politicians and businesses has led for some to a sense that the love of mammon has an unshakeable grip on society.

> In amazement the whole earth followed the beast. They worshipped the dragon, for he had given his authority to the beast, and they worshipped the beast, saying, 'Who is like the beast, and who can fight against it?' (Rev. 13.3–4)

> 'These are united in yielding their power and authority to the beast; they will make war on the Lamb, and the Lamb will conquer them, for he is Lord of lords and King of kings, and those with him are called and chosen and faithful.' (Rev. 17.13–14)

At such times it is difficult to feel that an agenda that puts 'the least of these' in the centre will triumph. This theme advocates an unmasking and naming of the 'principalities and powers' in the confidence that righteousness will reign.

If undertaking theological reflection is new, there are many books that introduce it and give guidance (see Appendix 4).

Riverford case study

Mrs Kaye asked the students whether, if they got more resources to meet their needs, that was fair on the rest of the school. Lee said, 'You are going to tell us there is a story about fairness in the Bible, aren't you? That's what we used to do in holiday club – whatever we did there turned out to be a story in the Bible about it.' Niamh said that she guessed what the story was going to be because her little sister had done it at Messy Church. It was the one about the man who was hiring people to work in his vineyard. The ones who only worked for part of the day got the same money as the ones who worked the whole day. 'But that's not fair,' said Michelle. 'But it is,' said Pete. 'You need to get the same GCSEs to go to college as the students who live in Holtbridge, but you don't get the same chance to study as they do.' Jane explained that the way they discussed this in meetings of the governing body was that you needed equality of opportunity if you were going to get equality of outcome. However, some people needed different opportunities because their circumstances were different, like living in Riverford rather than Holtbridge. So fairness couldn't mean treating everyone identically. 'I prefer the story,' said Mrs Kaye, 'it is easier to remember.' Pete said they should make it clear to the governors that they were worth helping just because they were students at the Academy and not because they might get better exam results.

7

Identifying Who You Need to Speak to and What You Will Ask

Coalham case study

The team agreed that what they wanted the Job Centre to do was recognize how expensive it was getting the bus from Coalham and so only ask people to come in once a week. John and Nick went back to the people they had interviewed and asked them if that would be an improvement, and they confirmed it would. They started drafting a letter to the Job Centre manager asking for a meeting. Mark said he'd been doing some more research, and Job Centres reported to district managers, who were described as being responsible for localism initiatives. Oona said that in the NHS 'initiative' was a code word meaning money to change things. They targeted their letter to the district manager, asking her to come to Coalham.

This chapter continues the process by identifying the person or people to whom the case for change needs to be made and finding out what authority they have to change things. It is about preparing to initiate or build upon an existing relationship by asking for change. It is about being specific about the change being sought and the moral and practical reasons for asking.

Who has the authority to change things?

Knowing what the team now knows about the nature of the injustice, it can be tempting to ascribe negative intentions to the person or people with the power to change things. However, it is worth considering other possibilities:

- they are unaware of the problem;
- they know of the problem and have tried to tackle it themselves and failed;
- they feel they lack the authority to get things changed;
- they know that the change would be unpopular with the people who would have to implement it and so have opted for what at the moment appears to be the line of least resistance;
- solving the problem would require the cooperation of colleagues or other agencies and they don't believe that cooperation will be forthcoming.

Keeping an open mind about the motivations of the people with the authority to change things can help build a relationship that allows them to share some of the credit for positive change. If the team are sincere in feeling they have no reputation to build, then it does little harm to share or hand over the credit for positive change, especially if it energizes the agency to make the change. A more conflictual approach may be necessary, and Chapter 9 discusses ways of taking that forward, but it should not be the starting assumption.

It can also be tempting to start by going in over the head of the person who seems able to resolve the injustice. Again this is to start with the assumption of resistance rather than willingness to cooperate. If the problem is one of implementation rather than system change, it can be helpful in sustaining a solution if it is identified and implemented by those closest to the problem. However, this is not to be naive about the fact that some large organizations deliberately structure their systems of redress to give the front-line person a small amount of discretion in the hope this will resolve the majority of problems. If the discretion available to that person is insufficient, the next step is to escalate things to identify who does have the necessary power to make meaningful change.

To work in this way is to adopt the principle found in Catholic social teaching (Hornsby-Smith 2006) of subsidiarity – that is, that decisions should be made as close as possible to the people affected by them. It is also to see building 'right relationships' with people who have power as a long-term investment in a community where citizens flourish because those with authority feel they are trusted to resolve injustices.

Working out who you need to approach means being aware both of how organizational hierarchies work and how organizations shape the discretion available to people at different levels of the hierarchy (Jaques 1991).

Identifying the level at which someone works may indicate some of the issues you will face when you try to make contact. Usually the more senior a person the more likely they are to have a gatekeeper (secretary, executive assistant, private office), who will control access to them and to what they see. Their email, post and telephone calls are likely to be intercepted so that only the communication that their gatekeepers feel is relevant reaches them. This is done to make their lives manageable, but it also means assessing the power that the gatekeeper has to block your access and using the required level of persistence to break through it. More junior people are likely to have protocols for referring requests 'up the line'. It is worth asking at every point of referral, 'Can you explain why you don't have the discretion to resolve this problem?' That will help you understand how power is distributed in the organization.

Understanding how discretion works is important if you are to reach the person or group who has the authority to make the identified change. No two organizations are the same, but the table opposite (Table 1) gives a sense of how discretion is likely to be distributed (Jaques 1991).

Discretion to deal with cases consistently but with some flexibility.	Front-line worker.
Discretion to make exceptions or deploy extra resources to resolve individual cases.	Supervisor or middle manager.
Discretion to amend systems and structures so they work better for an identified group of people.	Senior manager.
Discretion to review the remit of the agency to see if it should actively collaborate with external stakeholders.	Chief executive in consultation with governance structures.
Discretion to decide whether the remit of the agency should be changed, or its targets and funding be changed.	Governance structures in consultation with funders and commissioners of services.

Table 1. The distribution of discretion.

The higher the level of discretion you need access to, the more energy it is likely to take to make the appropriate contact and the more robust the case you will need to make. If you do not resolve the issue with the paid staff of the organization, then you will need to approach the governance of the organization. In a private company that would be the board, in a public agency the board or elected politicians who hold the agency to account, and in a voluntary organization the trustees. Who these people are should be evident from the organization's website or by requesting a copy of their annual report.

You may have come to the conclusion that the problem exists because of ineffective relationships between more than one agency. This will involve identifying the authority-holder in all the agencies concerned and whether they have existing mechanisms for working together. Where relationships between agencies exist it is good to see how the issue can be resolved through those existing mechanisms. Where they don't, you may have to make contact with the governance bodies for the agencies so they take seriously the need to review the remit of the agency with regard to this type of problem.

The New Labour administrations were active in setting up partnerships to engage with multi-agency problems. Some of those have fallen into disrepair as agencies have experienced more pressure on their funding. Where they exist, they can be a good way of raising an issue and finding collaborative solutions. Local voluntary sector infrastructure bodies such as Councils for Voluntary Service or Volunteer Centres usually have staff with a good working knowledge of local partnerships and how to make contact with them.

What are the limits of their authority?

Having identified the people with the authority and the level of discretion you need, it is necessary to think about other factors that may, either in reality or in their perception, limit how they exercise their authority (Grey 2013). This section describes the most common factors.

Back office/front office relationships

It is common for large organizations to separate staff into 'front office' staff, who deal directly with the public or the organization's customers, and 'back office' staff, who operate the systems and processes needed to deliver the service or authorize the resources that the front-line staff member needs. In a well-functioning organization a good deal of thought has been given as to how these two groups of staff work together so that from the 'customer' perspective it is a seamless experience. However, breakdowns in communication and cooperation are not unknown. They can be detected when front-line staff use 'blaming' language about other parts of the organization. 'I'd love to help you but our computer system won't let me do this.' 'I can see your problem but they wouldn't let me do that.' To challenge this blaming behaviour you need to identify the level of the organization that is responsible for coordinating the efforts of the back office and front office and make your case there (Wainwright 2009).

Regulation

Many of the services that people rely upon are regulated in some way. This is to ensure that risks to the service users are appropriately managed and that the practices of front-line staff are safe and professional. It can be helpful to appeal to a regulator when attempts to resolve an issue have failed, because they can look at the problem from a wider experience of how it is dealt with elsewhere and then enforce regulations.

However, there are some front-line staff who can use the requirements of the regulator to behave in an inflexible or officious way: 'I'd like to help but it is more than my job's worth.' It is worth testing these assertions to ensure that regulation is not being used inappropriately.

It is also worth bearing in mind that successive governments have used regulation to try to drive up the quality of services without thinking about whether the resources are available to deliver that level of quality. This is particularly true in care settings where increasing the ratio of staff to service users can improve the safety and quality of care but also raise the cost. Where a tension between regulation and cost is involved, it may be necessary to talk to those who allocate resources.

Targets

Sometimes the provision of a service may be shaped by the setting of targets, whether by the senior management, governance structures or funders of the service. The aim of these targets is to focus those delivering the service on what they are expected to prioritize and give service users an indication of what level of service they should expect. Knowing what targets are and whether they are being met can be helpful in holding a service to account.

However, it is difficult to measure services precisely and so targets can often create perverse incentives whereby staff focus on what is being measured and forget the individual needs of the real human being in front of them. Some injustices arise because managers are focusing staff on meeting targets rather than using their discretion to respond to the real need.

Conditionality

Many public services are provided to citizens with conditions attached. An example would be that children are entitled to attend mainstream schools as long as their behaviour does not disrupt the learning of other students. When the school reaches the end of its ability to manage disruptive behaviour, the student is excluded and asked to attend a different form of education. As the pressure on schools to achieve attainment targets has increased, so for many their tolerance of disruptive behaviour has decreased.

In the UK, the most controversial area of conditionality currently is that linked to welfare benefits. Conditions have been made more onerous, enforced more tightly and the consequences of not meeting them made more severe, including 'sanctioning', that is, stopping or reducing payments for a period. This has amounted to a shift in the social contract assumed to exist between the state and the claimant and has unsurprisingly caused disruption, distress and controversy.

In dealing with conditionality it is important to understand a number of things:

- the individual's understanding of the conditions and the consequences of not meeting them;
- the individual's ability to comply with the conditions;
- the discretion available to front-line staff to vary the conditions to reflect the reality of the individual's circumstances;
- to whom and how appeal for redress can be made and what will happen while this process is followed.

This is an area where distinguishing faulty implementation from a faulty system can be most difficult. It is where working with a case-work agency to see what the patterns of problems are is particularly helpful.

Supply chains

Many of the public services that people rely upon are now delivered by a contract, which public sector commissioners award to contractors who may be private or voluntary or, more rarely, public sector organizations. Increasingly, 'prime contracts' are being awarded to private or voluntary organizations to coordinate the efforts of a number of subcontractors to deliver a public service. It has long been common for private sector organizations to work through supply chains and franchisees, so the service user is dealing with a third party rather than the organization they are paying.

Where a problem is related to a supply chain it is necessary to work out the links in the chain and how they might be influenced. Contractual arrangements are usually regarded as commercially sensitive and so organizations in the supply chain may be unwilling to supply information about costs, targets, quality and responsibilities if they feel that information will give a commercial advantage to their competitors in future rounds of bidding. At the top of every supply chain are decision-makers who have decided that 'outsourcing' is the best way to deliver the service, and they need to know if the chain they have put in place is not delivering the service they specified.

Wicked problems

New Labour administrations popularized the use of the term 'wicked problems' for those social problems that no one agency was responsible for solving. They appointed 'Czars', with the authority to require relevant agencies to work together and provide services that tackled the problem. That approach has continued in a modified form with the 2010 Coalition government who, for example, appointed a Victims' Commissioner to hold the criminal justice system to account from a victim perspective.

There is often an elusive search for integration within organizations and coordination between organizations, with a belief that 'one more reorganization' will resolve the problems that repeatedly recur. More realistically, 'wicked problems' are managed by designing effective means by which the departments or agencies involved can collaborate and then monitoring that the collaboration is effective. If 'integrating mechanisms' are too elaborate, then agencies try to bypass them because they inhibit the 'real work' of the agency. If 'integrating mechanisms' are too light-touch, they can fail to command the respect of the front-line workers required to cooperate with them. A willingness to design, test, redesign and monitor is needed from the governance bodies of all the agencies involved. Integrating devices cannot compensate for any one of the agencies involved having inadequate resources. This is technical work that probably lies beyond the capacity of a justice-seeking team, but the team can be clear about what the problem is, the agencies that need to be involved and their determination to keep the issue on the table.

This section has painted a picture of a complex world which takes some decoding. This is an important element of justice-seeking. This complexity is operated by real human beings who should be able to give an account of what they do and why. Where they are confused, then complexity has spilled over into complication, and the need for better design is evident.

What is it you want them to do?

All the work done so far should now put the team in a position to decide what change they will ask for. It is helpful to summarize in writing three elements in preparation for deciding how to make contact. These are 'the ask', the supporting case, and the moral argument. If the approach is unsuccessful, it is then possible to analyse which of these three things is being challenged, in order to develop tactics to try again.

The 'ask'

The 'ask' is a shorthand term used by lobbyists to clarify the change they are seeking. The acronym SMART is often used to help people set objectives for a project. It can also helpfully be applied to deciding what to ask for.

- *Specific.* Asking for something specific that the team both thinks and feels will address the injustice means that the person being asked will need to be specific in their response. It also enables the team to discuss what modifications to the 'ask' might be accepted.
- *Measurable.* Asking for something that can be monitored will enable the team to check that the issue has been resolved.
- *Achievable.* It is important to ask for something that lies within the authority of the person being asked. If they say they have insufficient authority, then that can lead to questions about who needs to be approached next and how.

- *Realistic*. It is helpful to ask for something which seems to be possible within the existing resources of the organization being approached. If they respond that there are insufficient resources, then it is possible to ask who is able to provide further resources.
- *Time-bound*. It is important to set a timetable within which the request will be acknowledged and then within which a substantive response will be made.

The supporting case

All the research done in Chapter 5 needs drawing together in a way that is accessible and clearly supports the 'ask'.

The moral argument

The team need to be clear why they think the current situation is unjust and what are the moral arguments that underpin the supporting case and 'ask'.

How much of this material you share and at what point should become clearer as you decide how to make contact.

Riverford case study

Pete, Lee, Michelle and Niamh agreed that what they wanted to ask for was for the Riverford library to stay open until 5.30 p.m. on Monday, Wednesday and Thursday nights, rather than close at 3.30 p.m. They assumed this would cost more money, and so they wanted to ask the school governors to pay for it.

Mrs Kaye found out from the woman who ran the library that a decision like that would need to go to the head of Library Services in the county council offices. They decided to write and ask for a meeting. When they saw how that went they would then talk to the school governors.

They felt they had sufficient evidence from the survey of students on the bus and the exam data from the school to support their case. They agreed that the moral basis for the request was that all students deserved the same chance to succeed, so they would not accept any changes that were dependent upon improved exam results.

8

Making Contact

Coalham case study

To their delight the team received a prompt reply saying that the district manager would send her local initiatives coordinator to meet them and bring the Job Centre manager with her. John and Nick contacted the four parents they were in touch with and asked if they would come to the church hall and meet the visitors. Keith said that the food bank volunteers would ensure that there was a welcoming cup of coffee. Ian, John and Mark worked on a document that pulled together all that they had found out and what they were asking for. Oona and Nick were frustrated that they were going to miss the visit, because they would be at work in Scholarton. The team encouraged Nick to bring the Justice and Peace Group up to date.

The visit started with Keith showing the visitors how the food bank worked, so they understood how they first became aware of the problem. Leanne then introduced two parents who talked about the transport costs of getting to the Job Centre. Mark talked about his sanction. John then handed over the document and talked them through what they had found out and what they were asking for. The local initiatives coordinator said that they had some money to pay for laptops and broadband connections in villages that were remote from Job Centres and that they would be willing to try that in Coalham to see if it increased the number of jobs local people applied for. They asked

Ian if the church hall could be the venue. John said they needed some time to consider the offer and thanked them for visiting in person.

After discussion and consultation, the group agreed that this was worth trying for the three mornings a week when the church hall was already open. They told the Work Programme office manager, and he agreed that his clients could use this facility too for some of their job search and online courses.

Knowing what you want to say is one thing, knowing when and how to say it is another. Sometimes a well-thought-out message is lost because it takes the wrong tone, uses the wrong medium and is insufficiently aware of the priorities of the person receiving it. Sadly, modern communication technology has decreased attention spans and increased impatience with messages that do not hit the mark.

There will be situations where the team is seeking to communicate with someone with whom there is an existing relationship, and that will give clues as to the best way of making contact. When it is a 'cold call', careful planning is needed to communicate effectively.

If you need to contact an elected politician, there are two helpful websites that enable you to identify the appropriate people, the issues they cover and something of their political track record. They are called 'Write to them' and 'They work for you' and are in the Bibliography.

What is the best way to change hearts and minds?

The research undertaken so far should indicate if there is a need to change hearts or minds, or both. Written communication is good for communicating evidence and making a clear 'ask'. Helping someone understand the significance of an issue and how it affects people is usually best done face to face.

Sometimes the stakeholder analysis will have shown that another agency or person is in a stronger position than the team to draw the issue to the attention of the person with authority. Agree with that intermediary what role they will play and whether they will continue to be involved when contact has been successfully established. The intermediary may not have had contact relevant to the issue – for example, many local councillors, when they serve a term of office as honorary Mayor, invite a local minister to act as their chaplain. This builds a relationship of trust which the minister might be willing to use to offer an introduction and assure the councillor that the team's approach about the work of the council is sincere.

Some organizations indicate on their website how contact can be made. With others, a series of phone calls is needed to get contact details for the relevant person. Politicians, both local and national, often hold surgeries where their office is happy to make appointments to see constituents. Some are unwilling to use surgeries to have broader issues raised and so other means of contact will be needed. Sometimes the unexpected happens and one of the team comes across the person with authority in the course of doing something else. It is always good to have a first 'ask' prepared in case this happens, usually a request for a meeting or visit.

While email has become the most common initial form of communication, it is important not to underestimate the impact of a well-written letter. It gives a slightly longer word length and suggests that the matter is important because the person has taken the trouble to buy a stamp. However, there are some politicians and senior people who will only deal with electronic correspondence, and so it is sensible to follow up with an email attaching the letter.

The purpose of the initial contact is to secure sufficient of the person's time for them to understand the issue and the case you wish to make. A long initial email or letter may get put in a pending tray or delegated to a more junior person to attempt to answer. If you wish the person with authority to engage with you, then you are probably seeking a meeting or a visit. The next section looks at how both can be approached.

Making contact faithful and effective

In making contact as a group of Christians, it is important that the tone of the contact mirrors the way in which Christians aspire to treat each other. The list of the fruits of the Spirit provided by Paul in Galatians 5 is a good starting point: love, joy, peace, patience, kindness, goodness, faithfulness, humility and self-control. As Paul says, 'There is no law against such things' (v. 23). It can be a challenge to exhibit these characteristics in the face of injustice. Is there a place for communicating God's anger at injustice? There may well be (see further discussion in the next chapter), but it is not the starting point. If the aim is a fruitful relationship, then those seeking to build it need to show the fruits that they bring to relationships.

Visits: hospitality, reality, evidence

The easiest way to explain an issue and the impact it is having on the people affected by it is to invite the person with the authority to visit and see for themselves. Someone at a senior level will normally give a maximum of an hour for a visit and so it is important to think about the most effective way of using that hour.

There are three elements I look for in a visit leading up to the 'ask' – hospitality, reality and evidence. It is good to quickly establish the ethos of the organization or group being visited. This can be done by welcoming the visitor in the same way that a service user or guest would be welcomed. At some point it is helpful to offer simple refreshments as an ice-breaker to allow more informal conversations to take place. They allow the visitor to circulate, while giving others present something to do and a stimulus to chat. If it is possible to demonstrate the positive attributes of the people affected by the issue, that should also be considered – perhaps in making refreshments, taking the visitor on a tour of the building or displays of their work. To offer this type of hospitality is to acknowledge that we all feel awkward in unfamiliar social settings, and both visitor and visited will communicate more effectively if they have been put at ease.

The major part of the visit should be spent establishing the reality of the issue and how it affects people on a day-to-day basis. Where possible, people affected should be encouraged to speak for themselves and explain things from their perspective. Any part they have played in building the case, for example by gathering evidence, should be highlighted.

The visit should end with a short version of the case for support and a clear description of the 'ask'. The credibility of the team in having gathered and analysed evidence needs to be established so that the 'ask' is taken seriously. The full case for support and the 'ask' should be handed over in hard copy at the end of the visit. Before the visitor leaves they should be asked when they will respond and what form that response is likely to take.

Immediately after the visit an email should be sent thanking the person for visiting and attaching the full case for support and the 'ask', and reminding them politely of any commitments they made. If they were non-committal at the visit, then the follow-up email should ask what form of response they will make and by when. It is often the case that a visit will be followed up by an invitation to come and meet with relevant people to present the case and discuss possible ways forward.

When the team meet after the visit they should compare notes and identify what they learned. Where questions were asked that they couldn't answer, they should think about how they can be answered.

It is good to offer a private visit if this is the first time an issue has been raised. However, politicians often want local media to report on any visits they make and to be able to feature them on their website and social media channels. It is important to agree before the visit what media, if any, will be invited and whose job it is to brief them. It is rare that local media send a photographer, yet they often appreciate a good photograph, and so it is worth finding a volunteer with a decent camera and building time for a photo into the schedule. Politicians will usually want to feature a photo on their website, and so you need to be clear about how quickly they will receive the photo.

Meetings: listening, respectful, but firm

Meetings provide an opportunity to present the case for support and the 'ask', and to draw upon the moral rationale for the 'ask'. It is tempting to start with an extended presentation of the case, but that runs the danger of the person disengaging and starting to worry about the messages on their smartphone or the time of their next appointment. Senior and busy people will usually give a maximum of half an hour for a meeting and so it is necessary to plan effective use of time and who will speak when.

PowerPoint can be a helpful way of displaying evidence for discussion but it can also put participants into cinema mode and out of dialogue mode. In a short meeting the most important thing is to keep the conversation going. Avoid long speeches. Summarize information and ask short, focused questions. For example: Is this the sort of information you need to make a decision? Are there other factors you will need to take into account? Who else will need to be involved in the decision? Aim to get to the 'ask' at least ten minutes before the end of the allotted time. Ask for a response and, if an immediate one is not possible, ask for a commitment as to when a response will be made.

As with visits, follow up the meeting with a thank-you email to which the case for support and 'ask' are attached. Where an undertaking has been given, politely remind the person of that. Where it hasn't, ask for one.

It is worth thinking about whether there is an opportunity to thank the people who give access to the person with authority and support them. They will have done the logistics of setting up the meeting and visit, and if there is follow-up work to be done, they will have to ensure it is allocated to someone and chased up. Acknowledging their role in the process is a fruitful way of behaving.

As with any important event, someone needs to focus on getting the logistics right: parking, toilets, mobile phone contacts for all involved, arriving on time, making any access or dietary needs known, being crystal clear about the rendezvous point and taking the photo. It can help the team work effectively if one person concentrates on the logistics, freeing others to concentrate on the content of the session.

Don't be surprised if you are treated as an ally. Many people who work within the systems and structures that people rely upon do so because they have a keen sense of justice themselves. They want to do a good job and get frustrated when things don't work. The issue you are presenting may be one they have already wrestled with. The evidence you bring and the 'ask' you make may help them progress something beyond the obstacles that have previously stopped them. It is important to maintain your independence, but it is also sensible to pick up on suggestions as to how the case for support can be strengthened or the 'ask' refined to make it easier to take forward.

Understanding the political cycle

Making contact can be affected by where politicians and policy-makers are in the political cycle. It is worth knowing about how the political cycle works, so that influence can be appropriately tailored both locally and nationally, particularly when you return to an issue a number of times (see Figure 5).

Figure 5: Political cycle.

Both political parties and individual candidates for office publish manifestos that set out their intentions should they be elected. The process of compiling these manifestos usually has two phases, the private phase and the public phase. In the private phase, parties and candidates are usually seeking feedback on things as they are now and where the scope for reform lies. They are interested in new approaches and big ideas. If you have ideas for reform that go beyond the existing paradigm, this is the point to propose them. The public phase is when the party goes through whatever consultation mechanisms it has to solicit its members' views on the proposals. Some parties invite feedback from interest groups or knowledgeable individuals at this stage.

Election campaigns are a good opportunity to encourage the public to take into account issues that matter to you when deciding how to vote. In a country where debate of public policy is often carried out by relatively few people in a few media outlets and places on the web, it is an important moment to bring your concerns to wider attention. Candidates seeking votes are usually willing to have a discussion, and hustings can be arranged to ensure the debate is a public and balanced one involving all candidates. See Appendix 2, giving guidance on charity and electoral law.

Once an election has taken place, there may be a period in which a coalition is negotiated between parties and they have to set priorities and agree which parts of their programmes can be jointly implemented. Even if a single party is in power, they have to turn the good intentions of their manifestos into a set of priorities they can act upon. This again is a moment when ensuring that elected politicians understand the level of support for your issue is important. It is also the moment at which the detail of policies has to be thrashed out and where, again, some well-thought-through alternative ways of doing things may be positively received.

Central and local government and many public agencies have an obligation to consult the public if they intend to change things in a way that will materially affect people. There is an important difference between consultation and negotiation, but again, if invitations to consultation are ignored, it is possible for government to assume that the issues have low salience and can therefore be given a lower priority or fewer resources. Spotting consultations can be a bit of an art form but finding out where they are published on the websites of relevant agencies and checking regularly is diligent but important work. When seeking to understand why something isn't working it can be possible to find online or to request the consultation responses submitted and learn from them what alternatives were suggested previously.

When central or devolved government decides new legislation is needed there are a number of points at which that process can be influenced. However, it is technical work and challenging for a local group to undertake. The best way to influence legislation is to find a national charity or campaigning group that shares your concern and support them by providing evidence of what is happening in your community, case studies of how people are being affected and a sense of urgency that the issue is real and requires action. Your offer of help will be well received because national campaigns often struggle to obtain that credible local information. Usually, in parallel with the passing of important legislation and subsequent to the passing of the Act, civil servants will be engaged in writing guidance for those agencies that will need to implement the legislation. Civil servants can often be sympathetic to dealing with issues in the guidance that are too detailed to be dealt with in the legislation. Drafts of the guidance are often published on departmental web pages. Again this is a moment where the influence of those who have practical knowledge can be valued.

A key responsibility of politicians is to set priorities and allocate resources. There are always more things that could legitimately and beneficially be done than there are resources to support them. This makes the setting of priorities a key point in the political process where influence is exerted. There are arguments that are deployed to protect the interests of different groups. The most salient of these is that doing nothing will in the medium term prove to be more expensive than providing a service. A number of service-providing organizations now try to calculate their social return on investment (SROI Network 2012) to show how their service saves additional expense for other services and reduces future demand on those services. Another argument is that the same outcomes can be achieved more economically by working in partnership or providing the service in a different way. Very often groups will use emotion to press their point by providing case studies that illustrate the need they wish to see met and depicting the individual distress that will result from a reduced or closed service.

A significant proportion of public services is now provided as the result of a competition in which a number of organizations bid to provide the service. The people within central and local government and the NHS who run these competitions are called commissioners. They operate under rules that say what level of community consultation they are required to undertake before commissioning a service to ensure it meets the needs of the relevant population. Again this is a technical process but it is possible to ask that evidence from your group is taken into account before the commissioning process begins.

Accountability involves monitoring the implementation of services and both affirming good service and raising concerns where services fall short. Many local authorities have scrutiny committees that look at the strategy of the local authority and its implementation. The clerks of those committees are usually happy to receive evidence from people affected and those working with them about the quality of implementation.

In this section I have tried to show that there are many more points at which the democratic process can be influenced than just voting. It is sad that awareness of those points of influence is low, especially when those responsible for them are often crying out for evidence about how things really work. I don't underestimate the effort involved in finding out when and in what form influence can be exercised, but this is the work to which I hope some in the local church will feel called.

Following up

Controlled escalation and persistence

It is important to get to the right person before you make your case. If after the initial contact it is clear that the person is too junior to make the change you seek, then ask who it is you need to speak to and repeat the initial contact with them.

It is not unknown to be ignored or to be dealt with at a snail's pace. This is where persistence is your best friend. Faced with a senior person who refused to respond to our requests for contact, a member of my team phoned the junior person assigned to answer emails from the outside world on a weekly basis. They were soon on first-name terms and it became apparent that we would not stop phoning until they had engaged with us in a way that meaningfully addressed the problem. After two months of this we also made it clear that we would be contacting the politicians responsible for the governance of the organization and raising the matter directly with them. Fairly soon after that we were told that we were a 'stakeholder' and would be 'engaged with'. To be fair to the agency, the problem turned out to be more complicated than we had envisaged, involving both regulators and supply chains. However, our polite persistence meant that progress was made and chased on a regular basis.

Saying thank you

It is important to acknowledge every response promptly. Where the response offers further progress on the route to a resolution, show appreciation for what has been offered. Where there are gaps, don't be afraid to point them out. Where you need to escalate an issue, explain why you are doing so and thank the person for the steps they have tried to take.

Riverford case study

The head of Library Services said that he didn't have time to meet them, but if they put their request in writing he would have it looked at. This was disappointing, but they decided to put their case for support and request for extended library opening hours in writing. The letter that came back was even more disappointing. The reduced opening hours in Riverford had been the subject of a consultation that concluded six months ago. The costs of remaining open for an additional six hours would be £300 a week, a cost that could not be justified for a small number of additional users.

It was hard when people with the authority to change things didn't seem to listen. Jane suggested that they should make a presentation to the school governors. At least they would listen to them. Michelle said she'd see if she could find the consultation about reducing library hours on the council website.

When they met to prepare the presentation for the school governors, Michelle had found that the consultation responses were on the council's website and that nothing had been said about the needs of school students. She had also found that the councillor responsible for Library Services was the councillor for Holtbridge. Jane kicked herself – of course he was – and he belonged to the same golf club as her husband. She would talk to Mr Owen and see if the councillor could be invited to the meeting of the governing body.

The group worked hard on the presentation to the governing body. They decided it would have most impact if all four students spoke. Michelle prepared a PowerPoint presentation, so they kept to the time they were given and everyone knew who was saying what.

After the governors' meeting, Jane received a letter from the chair of governors saying that, after discussion with the head of Library Services, they would pay for two sessions a week for two terms and review whether it made a difference. Mrs Kaye offered to sit in the library for the additional hours it was open as a point of contact between the students, the library and the school. Michelle and Niamh worked on a letter to explain to the Riverford students what was on offer. Lee prepared thank-you letters to the chair of governors, Mr Owen, the councillor and the head of Library Services. All the team members signed them to indicate how important the issue remained to them.

9

Amplifying Your Voice

Coalham case study

The team decided to make an event of the installation of the computers in the church hall. Nick took a photo, which got into the local paper – a public reminder of the purpose of the computers. Mark helped Keith monitor the usage of the computers and verify the information that the district manager would receive to evaluate their impact. Keith also asked computer users how many visits on how many days they had made to the Job Centre or Work Programme office in Scholarton in the previous week. Leanne made sure that all the parents she worked with were aware of the availability of the computers and why they were there. Keith ensured his volunteers did the same with food bank clients. This information collecting, they now realized, would be needed in any future case for support they had to make.

Knowing why you need to turn up the volume

Before turning up the volume it is important that the team discusses why they think what they have done so far hasn't worked. This involves drawing together all the feedback both objective and subjective from the actions that were taken to make the 'ask'.

Have holes in the supporting case become evident, and, if so, can they be filled before trying again? Was the wrong person or people approached, and, if so, should the 'ask' be retargeted at someone else? Was the 'ask' unrealistic in some way, and so can it be modified in discussion with those affected by the issue? Once these possibilities have been contemplated and exhausted, then the moment may have come for turning up the volume and mobilizing wider support publicly.

It is likely that the difficulties that have brought the team to this decision will have stirred up emotions of anger, frustration and even powerlessness. It is important that the team share these emotions so that they can be communicated in a way that does not obscure the points they wish to make. It is an important part of any public communication that the team share what they have already done and how they feel about the fact it has not yet resulted in any change.

This chapter shows how additional pressure can be brought to bear on a system or structure or person that is not responding. The next chapter argues that what has been learned about the unresponsiveness of an organization is valuable evidence for arguing for wider system changes.

From lobbying to campaigning

It is easiest to understand the decision to amplify the voice of the team as a shift from lobbying to campaigning. When those who have the authority to change things have declined to do so or even refuse to listen, the next stage is to make them aware of the wider support for change and to hold them to account publicly for their decisions. This section talks through different options for amplifying your voice.

Websites and social media of the people who have not responded

Because digital technology and social media are relatively new, most organizations have dedicated people monitoring them and supplying content for them. Strangely, a question posted on a Facebook page, website or Twitter can meet with a swifter and more helpful response than something communicated privately by email or letter. This is because the people monitoring these sites tend to be communications professionals, who have an eye to the organization's reputation. The upside of this is that you can make an unexpected breakthrough. The downside is that you need to be ready to engage rapidly if this happens, and know exactly what you are asking for – a meeting or a visit, for example. It can be tempting to engage with social media earlier in the process, but you lose the advantage of having given the organization an opportunity to act privately first. It can be more difficult for them to use their powers of discretion generously and creatively if the first challenge they receive is in public via social media.

Petitions and public meetings

There are some issues where it can be useful to use a petition to signal to decision-makers that a sizable number of local people feel the issue should be addressed. There are now websites such as change.org that enable you to do this online, but be sure that this method does not exclude people for whom the issue is important. The Street Life website can also help you raise an issue at neighbourhood level. For very local matters, a public meeting may be a way of showing that there is support for the issue and inviting decision-makers to attend and answer questions. Having someone who is seen as neutral but who is confident in chairing public gatherings is important if the decision-maker is to go away both with information about the problem and understanding the strength of feeling.

Protesting and public symbolic actions

One way to attract the attention of the media is to do something that represents the issue and invite them to cover it. Here it is good to have someone with a creative mind who can think both what might attract attention and what those who support your issue might be prepared to do. A common symbolic action that churches are often involved in is to get a group of people to sleep out overnight to draw attention to the problem of rough sleeping. It is important that the protest does not enable the media to stereotype or scapegoat people affected by the issue. It is good to have leaflets available that explain to passers-by why the protest or action is taking place and what they can do to support the issue.

Civil disobedience

There are groups who feel that non-violent civil disobedience is necessary to make their point. These are usually groups who feel that they are consistently unable to get their points heard or where the law itself is seen as unjust. Anti-nuclear and environmental protestors are perhaps best known for this type of protest.

For some Christians this would be an unacceptable way to pursue an issue. For others it is part of challenging laws which, although democratically made, they see as unjust. For those considering it, it is important to take legal advice, to learn from people who have already used this method of protest and to consider carefully what the consequences are likely to be for those involved and whether or not they can bear those consequences. For example, what the consequences might be of arrest and obtaining a criminal record.

From local to national

Another important way of turning up the volume is to seek national or UK-wide attention for the issue that concerns you. There are a number of ways in which you can do this.

Involving your denomination

If your team has affiliations to a denomination, it is worth finding out if that denomination has people working at a national or UK level to influence politics (see Appendix 2). They will have ideas and contacts that will help you raise your issue nationally.

Some denominations have their own regional and national democratic processes which members can use to raise issues of concern. This may be a way of bringing your issue to the attention of the wider Church and seeing if others share your concern. These processes can be protracted and so you need to think about whether the change you are seeking is suitable for this or whether there are more general lessons you have learned which can be used to raise awareness.

If you belong to the Church of England, then you have access to bishops, 26 of whom currently have seats in the House of Lords. They are able to raise issues within Parliament both formally and informally.

National charities and campaigns

National charities and campaigns have already been mentioned as a potential source of expertise and information, but they can also be very ready to take up a local case as an example of the wider points they are trying to make. You need to be clear about how any information or stories you offer will be used and ensure that does not conflict with your purposes. No matter how helpful someone offers to be you still have the power to say 'no', if you are at all uneasy. Look at the organization's website before you make contact. Do you feel comfortable with the way in which it represents people? If they have press releases on their website, do you agree with the approach they take to your issue?

Asking your MP to raise it with the relevant government minister

Your local Member of Parliament or member of a devolved legislature should be willing to raise the issue and have ideas on who should be contacted. All Members of Parliament have the right to write to a minister raising a question and to receive a reply which they can pass on to their constituent. Some MPs, for some issues, will follow up the letter by speaking informally to the relevant minister with the aim of understanding what the scope for change might be. The advantage of a letter is that it gives the minister's officials a chance to respond privately and make use of the discretion available within their authority to change things. But, just as at local level, the change you seek may not be forthcoming.

Westminster Hall debates, adjournment debates, House of Lords oral questions

Members of Parliament at Westminster have their own mechanisms for turning up the volume. Many MPs realize that one way in which they can demonstrate to their constituents that they are doing a good job is to take up issues and campaign on them publicly. This involves them doing things at Westminster which put public pressure on ministers. They can request a debate in Westminster Hall, or an end-of-day adjournment debate, which a government minister must attend and respond to the questions they raise (search parliament.

uk). These debates often end with the minister saying they are open to further correspondence and discussion. For an MP to offer to do this, they will want to be confident that your case for support is well substantiated and that other MPs will have experience of the same or similar issues and so be likely to come along to the debate and join in. All these debates are televised either on the BBC Parliament channel or Parliament. tv. Even though they may happen at rather anti-social hours, local media can have their attention drawn to them and cover them. You can also use social media to circulate a link to the coverage.

The House of Lords is often dismissed because it is not democratically elected but it is most valuable when it acts as a chamber of experts. Peers have an opportunity to table oral and written questions which a government minister replies to. If a peer tables an oral question, it is likely to draw people into the chamber from a range of political views but with some expertise, and that is likely to put the minister under pressure to make or promise a substantive reply. Most contacts with peers will be likely to arise from contacting national organizations interested in your issue.

The transcript of debates in Parliament is called Hansard and is available online. If an issue you are working on has been debated, it can be a useful source of information and contacts.

The Westminster Parliament enables MPs and peers to form cross-party interest groups on any matter that they feel is important. The list of these interest groups can be found on the parliament.uk website. Their membership will indicate parliamentarians who have a declared interest in your issue. It is always good to make contact by post as well as email. Some parliamentarians have abandoned their official email addresses because they are so overwhelmed by online-generated emails that they can't identify who wishes to speak to them individually. If they have an assistant, it is good to make contact with them by email as they are likely to prioritize what their parliamentarian reads.

Working with the media

Print and broadcast media

The job of the media is to make public that which is in the public interest. However, most media channels will only pick up an issue if it can be made interesting to the public. In contemporary culture, that usually means bringing a problem to life by relating the experience of a real person. In addition, you need to be able to support that story with facts and figures. The same ethical and consent issues about using someone's story discussed in Chapter 5 apply even more. People need to be explicitly asked if they are willing for their story to be shared in the media and whether they are willing to be interviewed by a journalist. They need time to think through any possible adverse consequences and to take on board the fact that in this digital age what is said about them will be available for ever.

It is difficult to make effective use of any media that you don't regularly consume. The team should either themselves or through helpers monitor regularly the media outlets that are likely to cover the issue they are trying to raise. This enables you to be familiar with how they cover things, what length of material they will run and who their target audience is.

Local politicians and individual MPs follow their local newspapers closely because they are mainly read by middle-aged and older people who also tend to be most likely to vote. If an issue is raised in that context, they are likely to want to respond. Many local radio stations have at least one presenter who has a consumer or local issues focus, and they are often keen to be given an issue that they can use to hold someone in authority to account. However, local print and broadcast media tend to have very few journalists and so the material you offer them needs to be close to 'cut and paste'. Any press release needs to contain a factual statement of the situation which could be lifted into a news story or used to introduce a radio interview, as well as having a paragraph that gives your view of the situation.

What you make available needs to be concise and accurate. Don't submit anything longer than they are likely to use. Journalists won't have the time to precis it for publication. If you feel you have been misrepresented, don't hesitate to complain. All media outlets should have some means of acknowledging mistakes.

Most important is to work to their deadlines. Phone up to check exactly when they need to receive your material in order to make use of it. Realize that the closer to the deadline you submit, the busier they are likely to be. They are unlikely to have time to come back to you and check anything that was unclear to them. Submitting early gives you the best chance of coverage that meets your needs as well as theirs. Photos are always a help but must be of sufficient quality to go straight into the publication or be loaded on to a website.

National media tend to be looking for material that will illustrate a point they are trying to make. There is a greater danger that material you offer will be reshaped to make their point. Ideally any contact with national media should be done with the support of a media officer experienced in dealing with them (Richards 2005). If your team is part of a local church in a national denomination, there may well be protocols about contacting national media and media officers who can advise you. Media officers are there to help you get your point across and protect you from misrepresentation. There may be other people in your denominational structures who you feel you should inform. A good question to ask is, 'Who would I want on my side, if the situation escalated?'

Social media

Social media outlets vary greatly in each locality. Some communities have websites or blogs that are well read.[1] It is fine to ask what size the audience of any outlet has before you take

---

1 http://streetlife.com/ can be a good way of mobilizing people and then keeping them in touch with one another.

the trouble to prepare material for it. Most print and broadcast media now have online versions that invite the public to comment on articles. It is advisable to monitor these comments and respond to any that are factually wrong or that misrepresent the people affected by the issue. Get someone else to check what you have written before you press 'post' as it is easy to get drawn in by emotive language to exchanges of heat rather than light.

The UK has one of the highest proportions of its population online in the world and over half of pensioners are on Facebook (Lucas 2012). As with mainstream media, the advice is only to use social media that you already both consume and participate in. That existing experience will ensure that you use it in a way that is appropriately focused. If team members are going to use their existing online identities to increase awareness of the issue they are working on, they need to be comfortable that this will be accessible to the other people on their networks and that these are the people they wish to reach. By far the most popular social media platforms used for raising awareness of an issue at the time of writing are Facebook, Twitter and YouTube. Google+, Pinterest and LinkedIn are also significant but are less used for campaigning. As with all campaigning, it is important to start by thinking who you want to target and what you want them to do. Do you want them to indicate support of your issue by 'Liking' it on Facebook or YouTube, or retweeting your tweet? Do you want them to interact with you and give examples of the issue you are working on? You can create a page for your campaign on Facebook and use that to garner support, convey messages and get feedback.[2] You can shoot a short video and post it on YouTube.[3] However, because social media is fast moving, it is important to have someone on the team with the time to respond promptly. It is also worth thinking about who would be seen as influential by

---

2 There is an unmoderated Facebook page for this book so you can meet other people working on justice issues. Search 'Just Mission'.

3 About three minutes is seen as the maximum attention span for something well filmed, less if one person is talking straight to the camera.

the people you wish to reach with your campaign and target them. Their social media will give you an idea of how many friends or followers they have and so their potential to cascade your message. One thing is sure, that whatever is written about social media doesn't stay true for very long and could well be out of date between the writing and publication of this book.

This chapter has offered a wide range of tactics for amplifying your voice. It is unlikely that you will use them all, but being aware of the possibilities helps you focus your energies on things that seem both manageable and likely to get your message across to the people who you want to hear it.

Riverford case study

Jane invited the Holtbridge councillor and Mr Owen to come to the Riverside Library and have their photograph taken with the students in the week when the hours were extended. Lee took the photo and emailed it straight off and so managed to get it into the *Holtbridge Advertiser* and then on to the Academy and local authority websites. The councillor promised she would meet with the governors again when the review took place at the end of two terms. Mrs Kaye offered to keep a note of how many Riverford students used each extra library session, and Michelle offered to do a survey of students at the end of the first term. They realized that they had had a partial victory and that more data would be needed to build a future case for support. They agreed to meet again at the beginning of the school holiday.

10

Evaluating Your Impact

Coalham case study

On reflection, the group felt it had had an easy win with the Work Programme manager, but they had not got what they really wanted from the Job Centre. It had been easier to work with them to find ways round the rules rather than get the rules changed. John decided to meet with their MP when she next held her surgery in Coalham and talk her through the issues. With an election coming up, she needed to know that the service provided to Coalham residents by the Job Centre was a matter of local concern.

This chapter encourages the team to hold themselves to account by regularly reviewing the impact of their actions. In seeking to hold systems, structures and people to account, it is necessary to 'walk the talk' and be ready to give an account of the team's work.

Have they done what we asked?

The purpose of the justice-seeking activity has been to bring about change for those affected by the issue. That process has involved clarifying the issue, building alliances, building a case and asking for change. At the point at which a change is offered, the team is likely to feel excited that their work has borne some fruit. While not suppressing the excitement, it is important to step back and evaluate whether what is being offered is what is needed and whether it is acceptable to those affected by the issue. This is a difficult moment because it is also important to hear the reasons given for the offer made. There may be a case for compromise so that something is done to remedy the injustice, or there may be a case for asking again for what is really needed. These are difficult judgements, and where they materially affect the well-being of people at the heart of the issue, their views must be of primary importance.

These decisions call for discernment, which again will draw upon the spiritual gifts of the team, their ability to communicate the offer and then listen to those affected by the issue.

Compromise can be seen as a dirty word. However, large organizations often find it easier to make an initial offer and then build on that, rather than give everything that is asked for. If the offer is accepted with a clear understanding that it is the beginning of a partnership to work for a full resolution, then it can be a constructive way forward. However, that is different from being fobbed off with something that is a token gesture and is designed to close down the conversation rather than open it up.

It is important to acknowledge promptly what is being offered. It will have taken effort and negotiation from those with the authority to make this offer, and that effort needs to be acknowledged, even if the offer itself is not immediately acceptable.

What if they have not done what we have asked?

It may be that even after turning up the volume or taking the local issue to a national level, a suitable response is still not made.

Accepting that all the efforts the team has made have not resulted in changes that will remedy the injustice is both an emotional and a spiritual challenge. It is natural to feel angry and despondent. It is also understandable to question God and with the Psalmist wonder why injustice persists. It is healthy to express these things as a cry to the missional God, who is also just in character. This book has worked from a starting assumption that not every Christian holds, that in a democratic society the system is open to challenge and that it is possible for injustices to be put right. Faced with failure, it will be natural for some to feel that nothing can be done because it is the system that is broken.

The spiritual challenge at this moment of anger and frustration is to continue to believe in the validity of challenging injustice. Failure can trigger diffidence where the team feel that they have been put in their place and don't have the right, obligation or capacity to speak out. Failure can also trigger an arrogance that comes from feeling slighted or belittled. Finding a place of humility from which to persist because of a mission that is shaped by God's character rather than our own status takes courage.

It may not be possible at first, but the team should regroup and try to identify what it has learned from the failure. It may be that new strategies are generated from this analysis and so a fresh 'ask' can be prepared or a different organization or person in authority approached. It may be that in going back to key stakeholders, a broader alliance for tackling the issue becomes evident. It sounds tiring, but justice often requires persistence. This may be a moment to involve some new people in the team and get them to take a fresh look at what you are doing. This type of accountability can sometimes make people feel defensive about the decisions they have made and the effort they have put in.

It can be tempting to keep fighting battles that have been lost. The case has been built and the 'ask' agreed, making it hard to decide when to stop and to try something different. If the refusal has been firm, then it is necessary to return to those affected by the issue and work with them to monitor the implications of this decision. If the issue has been about continuing or extending something or stopping something, then there will be repercussions of the refusal. Indeed, new people may be affected or the same group of people affected in different ways or with greater seriousness. Seeing this process as a spiral means that the refusal puts the team in a new position, with a new 'why question' to ask.

This is also a moment for reflecting upon the answers given to check they are unjust and not just answers we don't like. If resources are scarce, it may be that no matter how good your case, there are other problems that are more pressing. Are there different sources from which resources could come? Does the profile of the issue need to be raised so it becomes a genuine public priority for greater resources?

An advantage of working as a team is that it is possible to discuss energy levels and emotional and spiritual reactions. It should be easier to discern when getting an outsider to listen and reflect with the team would be beneficial.

Have we fed back to those affected by the issue the results of our actions?

Whether the 'ask' has met with success or failure it is vital to feed back the results of your actions.

Part of the decisions you made in how to work as a team (Chapter 4), and the listening you did in building the case (Chapter 5), will have been decisions about how your work would relate to those directly affected by the issue. Decisions about how to represent their stories and data will have required you to honour the commitments you made. It may be that your issue has involved regular contact with those affected, and so they will be receiving regular updates on your actions and the results of them. In the best case, some of those affected will have been part of the team. However, it may be that they have used advice agencies to pursue their individual cases and have been glad for the team to tackle the wider issue. Whatever the issue, your first accountability is to those directly affected and they need to understand what you have done and what results your action has had.

This communication needs to be done in a timely way and in a format that they find accessible. Most people need to receive important information in more than one format so they can fully absorb it. Often a written communication (letter, email, leaflet) followed by a chance to ask questions (telephone, meeting, one to one) helps.

If you have worked with other stakeholders or benefited from the input of other organizations, this is the moment to give them feedback on the results of your efforts.

What to do with evidence that those in power are not behaving accountably

As the last chapter discussed, you may come across situations where those with power are not willing to give an account of their actions and are resistant to the additional pressure you have brought to bear by turning up the volume.

It is worth checking that you have exhausted any complaints procedure that the organization operates itself. There are some areas, such as health, where it is acknowledged that complaint systems are confusing and can pass people from one point to another (Healthwatch England 2014). Where this is the case it is worth looking at who might be able to offer support in making a complaint (see Citizens Advice website).

When this is done it is a good idea to look at whether the person or organization with the power is accountable to an ombudsman or tribunal or whether the issue you are raising is regulated (see Bibliography for websites).

Not all these services of redress are free to those making the complaint. While all these services are designed to be used by ordinary citizens, some of them can be daunting and take on a quasi-legal process. At the point at which you feel out of your depth you need to go to a relevant local advice agency for help and in addition set out the obstacles you face to your Member of Parliament.

If you can't beat them, join them

Involvement in a justice-seeking process is likely to make you aware of how dependent upon good advice and good governance a society is if it is to be a just society. It is not uncommon for this sort of process to evoke a vocational impulse to be part of the structures that shape people's lives, or take on responsibility for holding them to account. Christians are already well represented in politics, governance and the advice sector, but there is always a need for the next cohort to step forward and get involved.

Elective politics for Christians

There is an organization called Christians in Politics (see Bibliography) that is dedicated to informing Christians about how they might get involved in elective politics and putting them in touch with other Christians who have followed this path.

Governance for Christians

Becoming a school governor, a trustee of a local charity or a board member of a public sector agency or private company can all be ways of ensuring that organizations that serve local communities are accountable and consider justice in their deliberations.

There are a number of important voluntary roles that citizens can play in the criminal justice system, for example, magistrates, members of youth offending panels, prison visitors, police station visitors and members of restorative justice panels.

Advocate for advice agencies

Churches are often very generous in fundraising and giving to support local charities. Hopefully the experience of justice-seeking will make you aware of the often unglamorous and unsung work of the advice sector and the need that it has for both donations and volunteers. It may not have the same emotional pull as other causes, but a church committed to justice-seeking will ensure it finds a place in the causes they support. Often it is not so much the size of the donation but the fact that the agency can point to unsolicited community support that makes it better able to apply to other sources of funding.

This chapter has sought to draw together the threads of the justice-seeking process and show how it is in fact a cycle with both success and failure giving rise to new questions.

Riverford case study

On reflection, the team felt that the initial negative response from the head of Library Services could have stopped them in their tracks. It was having the opportunity to make a presentation to the school governors that meant that they got some of what they had asked for. Pete said that it made him realize that you mustn't be afraid to keep on asking. Lee said, 'I bet you Mrs Kaye has got a story about that too.'

Conclusion

Being Changed as Well as Seeking Change

Coalham case study

Ian's boss asked him to think about what sort of jobs he would apply for at the end of his curacy and what he would say to the bishop about where he would be willing to work as a priest with his own parish for the first time. Ian realized that if he had been asked that question after his first six months at Coalham he would have described somewhere like Scholarton! Now he could see that his vocation was developing to places like Coalham that were on the edge. John's reflection was that his friendship with Ian meant that he now saw church as more than 'for the wife'. It had been good to encourage a young man starting out in his ministry, and he could see that there were ways of making a difference. He asked Leanne whether she thought the group's work was done. Leanne said, 'This is just the start. I have at least half a dozen questions I'd like to see tackled. We were hoping that you would lead us on.'

This book started from the position that justice-seeking was an activity of the Church because justice is a characteristic of God. At the end of the process it is worth reflecting upon how justice-seeking has changed the churches and people involved. A key element of mission is that in being sent by God into the world to collaborate in his purposes, we ourselves will be changed as well as seeking to bring about change. This Conclusion looks at the ways in which we are changed through three lenses: discipleship, evangelization and apologetics.

Just mission as discipleship: forming Christ-like people

Discipleship is a process of learning. As this book has shown, justice-seeking involves a constant process of learning about the reality of people's lives, the systems and structures that shape their lives and our own responses to the moments of discernment, success and failure that are part of the process. Hopefully, some of the moments of discernment have resulted in the team engaging with the Christian tradition to ensure right discernment and an ethical basis for their decisions that they can articulate to themselves and to others. This may not be the type of discipleship learning offered within courses or Bible studies but it may be an approach to learning that engages those whose learning is triggered by experience or who need to ask 'Why?'

Discernment as risk-taking stewardship

The justice-seeking process can help a local church discern talents and abilities it might otherwise have overlooked. In Holtbridge, Irene approached Jane because she felt she might be the person to solve a problem. In turn, Jane approaches Mrs Kaye because she holds the keys to Riverford Chapel. In reality, both women are able to support each other in working with the students. In Coalham, Ian approaches John because he saved him from social embarrassment and included him in his group of friends. In reality, John has facilitating skills that allow a group of Anglicans, Roman Catholics and people connected to the food bank and school to work together. These moments of discernment are often fleeting, but they involve putting trust in others. Being trusted can both affirm and change people.

Integrating hand, heart and head

The learning that takes place as part of justice-seeking develops interdependence and integration. It is evident that those who start with the head need those who start with relationships and those who start with action. Each could gain a greater appreciation of the other. Equally this experience of interdependence should evoke awareness of those aspects of our personality that come less readily to the fore. As the Enneagram approach to spirituality suggests, these predispositions are strengths we can build on, not straitjackets that constrain us.

It is good to reflect both as a team and individually on the ways in which the process of justice-seeking has changed us. Discipleship is a journey, and identifying the milestones can help set future directions.

Just mission as evangelization – making the Church more gospel-shaped

If the local church is to grow, it needs to be a compelling reflection of the God it seeks to bear witness to. Justice-seeking will reshape the Church, so that it achieves a better likeness to the God of justice. Bevans and Schroeder (2004) offer a useful metaphor for this:

> Lesslie Newbigin speaks persuasively of the local Christian congregation as a 'hermeneutic of the gospel', meaning that it is oftentimes only in the local community where the gospel is truly lived that people encounter what the gospel is really about. (p. 354)

Worship, learning, healing, hospitality and fellowship as acts of justice

I see significant potential in justice-seeking for making the local church more gospel-shaped. Justice-seeking may extend the resources used in worship to allow greater contemplation of God as just, and the expression of emotions such as anger and grief at the injustices of the world. Learning may take on a new urgency as questions from the reality of the local community are brought to the Christian tradition and what is learned from the tradition affects the questions that are asked about the community. Pastoral care will still have the aim of bringing healing and reconciliation but it will provoke questions about why the needs expressed are there. Hospitality will become more focused on including people who feel excluded from other gathering places in the community and encouraging people to journey from guest to host in providing a welcome on behalf of the Church. Fellowship may become a focus for integrated mission as those parts of the body with different gifts express their interdependence and tensions are explored rather than suppressed. This reshaping is not the work of a moment, or even of a single cycle of justice-seeking, but it carries the seeds of change.

The Church as a just community

The listening that is required in the process of justice-seeking increases sensitivity to who is being heard and whose views are being sought in any situation. This sensitivity can then lead to a desire to make the churches we belong to places of greater listening where everyone has a voice. What are the rhythms and routines of the local church that enable people to have their say and express their hopes and desires for the development of the life of the church? Whose voices are missing from deliberations about mission?

Just mission as apologetic: explaining the gospel to the world

In a society that no longer assumes that it is Christian and where many voices compete to influence politics, the Church needs to find ways of explaining itself that are accessible and vivid. Justice-seeking can be part of that explanation, engaging with the world on its own terms but asking for change on the basis of a Christian ethic and belief.

If justice-seeking becomes part of the practice of the local church, it becomes part of its story, a story that is both public and theological. The stories the local church tells may be about details that may fall beneath the notice of proper theology, but the gospel suggests that, like sparrows, they are not beneath God's notice. The integrated mission approach, bringing together compassion, righteousness and justice, results in what Clemens Sedmark (2003, p. 130) has called 'little theologies' that are evoked by burning questions and found to be empowering in the context for which they are developed. My experience of working with colleagues looking at churches' work in London is that reflecting on collections of these stories can give fresh insights into the Church and the world (Cameron et al. 2010).

For some this will seem too bold an approach, insufficiently conscious of the abuse that has taken place in the name of the Christian tradition (Walton 2014, Chapter 15). For others, this local approach may seem too timid, and lack the visibility required to speak truth to power (Graham 2013; Bennett 2013, Chapter 9). Our culture is suffused with stories both in the media and in fiction that make a point by describing human experience in vivid detail. For me, the challenge for a local public theology is knowing what the point of the story is and ensuring its implications for church and society are explored. This is not about applying high-level principles to low-level problems. It is about seeking the character of God in the stuff of everyday life and finding something priceless.

Riverford case study

Mrs Kaye reflected that the fruit of her earlier work with the holiday club was still there in the young people of Riverford and that, although she had less energy, sitting and listening was still of value.

Jane had been impressed and surprised at the impact that the Methodist Holiday Club had had in Riverford. She described what she had learned to Irene and asked her to think about whether there was anything the circuit could do for children in Riverford. Jane had not forgotten that the original impetus for the group had come from Niamh's family moving into emergency accommodation in a former council house on the edge of Riverford. Jane knew about the local property market from the conveyancing she did as a solicitor, but it had not occurred to her that there were significant numbers of families in Holtbridge who were struggling to get permanent affordable accommodation. Looking further afield, she realized this was also true of the village where their weekend cottage was. They could let it out as a permanent home at an affordable rent, and it would still be there as an asset when they retired. After discussion with her husband, Jane contacted a letting agent. Jane reflected that she no longer felt so trapped in Holtbridge – all human life was there, and there were people like her, trying to do a good job, who could do more if they knew each other better. Coffee after church on a Sunday morning had become an opportunity to listen differently.

Appendix 1

Being Political while
Staying within the Law

This appendix points you to sources of guidance on the laws in the UK affecting the political activity of charities.

In the UK, churches are usually registered as charities, either at the level of the local church or as part of a denomination, and sometimes as both. There are two types of law that affect what charities can say in public: charity law and electoral law.

This is not legal advice, but tries to put it in a nutshell. Charities can be 'issue political' but not party political. They can speak out about the issues that are relevant to their objectives, as long as they don't do so in a way that supports a particular political party. Charities can be controversial, but they must be able to back up anything they say with facts and evidence. In the period running up to an election, charities must be particularly careful not to act in a way that could be seen as lending their support to a particular political party or candidate.

In other countries, churches sometimes have a wider range of legal forms they can adopt. The law on freedom of speech for churches also varies. However, the principles of exercising influence in a transparent way and being able to support statements with evidence are helpful in any context.

Charity law

Charity Commission Guidance

Speaking Out: Guidance on Campaigning and Political Activity by Charities (CC9), available at www.gov.uk/government/publications/speaking-out-guidance-on-campaigning-and-political-activity-by-charities-cc9.
The document has a helpful overview.

NCVO good practice

http://knowhownonprofit.org/campaigns/campaigning.
NCVO is the membership organization for charities in England. It publishes advice on lobbying and campaigning.

Scottish Charity Commission

www.oscr.org.uk/hot-topics/political-campaigning-guidance-for-charities.
There is a separate charity commission for Scotland that publishes its own guidance.

Electoral law

Things churches can do during elections

Voter registration

www.electoralcommission.org.uk/i-am-a/voter.
See this for information on how to register to vote. Those people who are particularly at risk of not being registered are young people, those who have moved address in the six months running up to the election, those who are in insecure accom-

modation or homeless and those who have difficulty with forms and complicated letters.

Raise issues with candidates

Candidates standing for election are keen to meet as many voters as possible to communicate their policies. Voters need the opportunity to question candidates about their policies should they be elected. Churches often have groups of people meeting in them who would welcome the opportunity to meet candidates. Provided all candidates are given the opportunity to visit, then this activity is not regulated within electoral law.

Raise issues with the public

Charities often wish to bring to the attention of the public in the run-up to an election public policies that they think would benefit the people they serve. When doing this it is important to think about whether the tone and approach could be seen as encouraging the public to vote for a particular candidate. Guidance on electoral law can be found below.

Hold hustings

A hustings is a meeting where election candidates or parties debate policies and answer questions from the audience. Hustings provide voters with an opportunity to hear the views of candidates or parties. They often have a similar format to *Question Time* or similar programmes broadcast on television. The Electoral Commission provides guidance on how they are to be run. Provided their rules are followed, hustings are not regulated activities under electoral law.

Electoral Commission

www.electoralcommission.org.uk.
See the section on non-party campaigners. Remember that the law can change between elections and there are different rules for different types of elections. It is a good idea to check the website if you are within six months of an election or referendum.

Churches Together in Britain and Ireland

www.ctbi.org.uk.
This website usually has guidance on holding hustings and other material helpful to churches in the period prior to EU, UK and national elections within the UK. It is common practice in the UK for local groups of churches to work together to hold a hustings.

Appendix 2

Working with Denominations and Agencies

Denominational information

- Church of England: In the first instance contact your diocesan social responsibility officer but see the policy work done nationally at https://www.churchofengland.org/our-views.aspx. To follow what Church of England bishops say in the House of Lords, go to http://churchinparliament.org/.
- Church of Scotland: www.churchofscotland.org.uk/speak_out.
- Church in Wales: www.churchinwales.org.uk/society/.
- Catholic Church in England and Wales: www.cbcew.org.uk/CBCEW-Home/Legislation-Policy; see also www.justice-and-peace.org.uk.
- Catholic Church in Scotland: www.rcpolitics.org; see also www.justfaith.org.uk.
- Caritas Social Action Network: www.csan.org.uk/advocacy/.
- Joint Public Issues Team – works on behalf of the Methodist Church, the Baptist Union of Great Britain and the United Reformed Church – www.jointpublicissues.org.uk/.
- Methodist Church: www.methodist.org.uk/mission/public-issues.
- Baptist Union; www.baptist.org.uk/Groups/220639/Engaging_with_Society.aspx.
- United Reformed Church: www.urc.org.uk/mission/church-and-society.html.

- The Salvation Army: www.salvationarmy.org.uk/politics-policy.
- Quakers: www.quaker.org.uk/public-issues.
- Unitarians: www.unitarian.org.uk/pages/social-justice.

Other agencies

- Scottish Churches Parliamentary Office: www.actsparl.org/.
- Cytûn (Churches Together in Wales): www.cytun.org.uk/churchandsociety.html.
- National Church Leaders Forum: A Black Christian Voice: www.nclf.org.uk.
- CARE: www.care.org.uk/advocacy.
- Evangelical Alliance: www.eauk.org/current-affairs/politics/.
- Churches' Legislation Advisory Service: www.churches legislation.org.uk.

Appendix 3

Reading the Book in a Small Group

This appendix guides a small group in reading the book over six sessions.

Group members need to read the relevant chapters in preparation for each session. The Bible passage for each session needs to be made available during the session.

The format for the session could follow that of an existing small group or the format suggested below could be adopted.

Feedback from some readers of the book is that Chapter 2 is the most challenging to understand. For some groups it may make sense to reorder the sessions and have Session 2 as the final session.

Session plan

- Prayer.
- Bible reading and contemplation of its relationship to justice.
- Discussion of pre-reading to ensure shared understanding.
- Discussion of the two questions.
- Reread Bible passage.
- Prayer.

Session contents

Session 1

Pre-reading: Introduction and Chapter 1.
Bible passage: Micah 6.6–16.
Discussion questions:
- How do you think politics is changing?
- Where might questions of justice arise in the life of your community?

Session 2

Pre-reading: Chapter 2.
Bible passage: Luke 24.13–35.
Discussion questions:
- How can disciples disagree but still walk together?
- Who has power in our community, and how accountable are they?

Session 3

Pre-reading: Chapters 3 and 4.
Bible passage: Matthew 20.20–28.
Discussion questions:
- What are the injustices in Coalham and Riverford?
- Should Jane have been clearer about whether she was acting as a school governor or church member?

Session 4

Pre-reading: Chapters 5 and 6.
Bible passage: Matthew 20.1–16.
Discussion questions:
- Do you think Oona jumped the gun by calling in at the Job Centre?
- Is there a tension between Jane's and Pete's views of the story of the labourers in the vineyard?

Session 5

Pre-reading: Chapters 7 and 8.
Bible passage: Matthew 15.21–28.
Discussion questions:
- Do you think the offer made to the Coalham team dealt with the question they started with in Chapter 4?
- Was Jane justified in using a personal contact to persuade the councillor to attend the governors' meeting at Holt-bridge Academy?

Session 6

Pre-reading: Chapters 9, 10 and the Conclusion.
Bible passage: Matthew 21.12–17.
Discussion questions:
- Are there limits to what Christians should do to make their point?
- Is there a 'why question' or burning issue emerging in the group?

Appendix 4

Further Reading

This book is written in a style that will be accessible to people in local churches wishing to think about justice.

However, the book is also intended for those preparing for public ministry or seeking to develop their practice through formal study. This Appendix suggests some further reading that may help with this purpose.

Starting point

Surprisingly for a topic that is so connected to the real world, a lot of the theological writing relating to politics is written in abstract and dense language. For me, the book that most helpfully provides a map of the territory and sign posts key authors is by Elizabeth Phillips: E. Phillips, 2012, *Political Theology: A Guide for the Perplexed*, London: Continuum. Elizabeth Phillips divides the field into three main clusters of writing: political, liberation and public theology. For each I have suggested a 'companion' book that brings together essays outlining the field. These are large and expensive books, and so you may need to track them down in a library. I have also suggested some authors who for me offer an accessible way in and then an academic journal that carries relevant articles.

Political theology

Companion book: P. Scott and W. T. Cavanaugh (eds), 2004, *The Blackwell Companion to Political Theology*, Oxford: Blackwell Publishing.

Key authors: Luke Bretherton, Peter Scott, Graeme Smith.

Journal: *Political Theology*.

Public theology

Companion book: W. F. Storrar and A. R. Morton (eds), 2004, *Public Theology for the 21st Century*, Edinburgh: T & T Clark. There are two books that provide helpful overviews as well as making a contribution to the current debate: E. Graham, 2013, *Between a Rock and a Hard Place: Public Theology in a Post-Secular Age*, London: SCM Press; M. Brown (ed.), 2014, *Anglican Social Theology*, London: Church House Publishing.

Key authors: Christopher Baker, Jonathan Chaplin, Elaine Graham, Nick Spencer.

Journal: *International Journal of Public Theology*.

Liberation theology

Companion book: C. Rowland (ed.), 2007, *The Cambridge Companion to Liberation Theology*, Cambridge: Cambridge University Press.

Key authors: Christopher Rowland, Andrew Bradstock.

Journal: The previously mentioned journals would also cover this field.

Theological reflection

A book of this length and style cannot cover in detail two foundations upon which the material rests, namely, theological reflection and the UK political context. Again, I recommend some ways into the topics and a journal that carries relevant articles.

For me, Judith Thompson's book remains the most helpful introduction to theological reflection: J. Thompson with S. Pattison et al., 2008, SCM *Studyguide to Theological Reflection*, London: SCM Press.

For a worked example, linking theological reflection to issues in local public theology, see H. Cameron, J. Reader et al., 2012, *Theological Reflection for Human Flourishing: Public Theology and Pastoral Practice*, London: SCM Press.

The Salvation Army, with assistance from Judith Thompson, has produced a practical guide to facilitating groups. The resource can be downloaded from their website in a number of languages and with accompanying tools: www.salvationarmy. org/fbf.

Journal: *Practical Theology*.

The UK political context

Here are four books that give an accessible way into the political context.

G. Stoker, 2006, *Why Politics Matters: Making Democracy Work*, Basingstoke: Palgrave Macmillan. Although this book predates current shifts in UK politics, it provides a thoughtful guide to the steps needed to reanimate democracy and a helpful analysis of localism.

J. Hills, 2015, *Good Times, Bad Times: The Welfare Myth of Them and Us*, Bristol: Policy Press. This is a good summary of the condition of the UK welfare state underpinned by lots of evidence.

I. Newman, 2014, *Reclaiming Local Democracy: A Progressive Future for Local Government*, Bristol: Policy Press. Ines Newman provides a thoughtful reflection on the problems and potential of local government; it is written for practitioners.

H. Wainwright, 2009, *Public Service Reform ... But Not As We Know It! How Democracy can Transform Public Services*, Hove: Picnic Publishing. Written like a novel, this book gives an insider view of what is involved in bringing about change in complex organizations.

Journal: *Policy and Politics*.

Bibliography

Atherton, J., C. Baker et al., 2011, *Christianity and the New Social Order*, London: SPCK.

Baker, C., 2007, *Hybrid Church in the City: Third-Space Thinking*, Basingstoke: Ashgate.

Bennett, Z., 2013, *Using the Bible in Practical Theology: Historical and Contemporary Perspectives*, Farnham: Ashgate.

Bennett Moore, Z., 2002, *Introducing Feminist Perspectives on Pastoral Theology*, Cleveland, OH: The Pilgrim Press.

Bevans, S., 2002, *Models of Contextual Theology*, Maryknoll, NY: Orbis Books.

Bevans, S. B. and R. P. Schroeder, 2004, *Constants in Context: A Theology of Mission for Today*, Maryknoll, NY: Orbis Books.

Bickley, P., 2014, *Good Neighbours: How Churches Help Communities Flourish*, London: Theos and Church Urban Fund.

Bishop, G., 2007, *Darkest England and the Way Back In*, Leicester: Matador.

Bosch, D. J., 1991, *Transforming Mission: Paradigm Shifts in Theology of Mission*, Maryknoll, NY: Orbis Books.

Bretherton, L., 2010, *Christianity and Contemporary Politics: The Conditions and Possibilities of Faithful Witness*, Oxford: Wiley-Blackwell.

Brown, M. (ed.), 2014, *Anglican Social Theology*, London: Church House Publishing.

Cameron, H., 2010, *Resourcing Mission: Practical Theology for Changing Churches*, London: SCM Press.

Cameron, H., 2012, '"Life in all its Fullness" Engagement and Critique: Good News for Society', *Practical Theology* 5:1, pp. 11–26.

Cameron, H., D. Bhatti et al., 2010, *Talking about God in Practice: Theological Action Research and Practical Theology*, London: SCM Press.

Cameron, H., J. Reader et al., 2012, *Theological Reflection for Human Flourishing: Public Theology and Pastoral Practice*, London: SCM Press.

Catholic Bishops' Conference of England and Wales (CBCEW), 2008, *Choosing the Common Good*, Stoke-on-Trent: Alive Publishing.

Chaplin, J., 2009, 'Conclusion: Christian Political Wisdom', in N. Spencer and J. Chaplin (eds), *God and Government*, London: SPCK.

Davie, G., 2002, *Europe: The Exceptional Case – Parameters of Faith in the Modern World*, London: Darton, Longman & Todd.

Davis, A., D. Hirsch et al., 2014, *A Minimum Income Standard for the UK in 2014*, York: Joseph Rowntree Foundation.

Dean, H., 2010, *Understanding Human Need: Social Issues, Policy and Practice*, Bristol: Policy Press.

Gillham, B., 2008, *Developing a Questionnaire*, London: Continuum.

Graham, E., 2013, *Between a Rock and a Hard Place: Public Theology in a Post-Secular Age*, London: SCM Press.

Grey, C., 2013, *A Very Short, Fairly Interesting and Reasonably Cheap Book about Studying Organizations*, London: Sage.

Hallsworth, M., S. Parker et al., 2011, *Policy Making in the Real World: Evidence and Analysis*, London: Institute for Government.

Healthwatch England, 2014, *Suffering in Silence: Listening to Consumer Experiences of the Health and Social Care Complaints System*, London: Healthwatch England.

Hebden, K., 2013, *Seeking Justice: The Radical Compassion of Jesus*, Winchester: Circle Books.

Heywood, D., 2011, *Reimagining Ministry*, London: SCM Press.

Hills, J., 2015, *Good Times, Bad Times: The Welfare Myth of Them and Us*, Bristol: Policy Press.

Hornsby-Smith, M. P., 2006, *An Introduction to Catholic Social Thought (Introduction to Religion)*, Cambridge: Cambridge University Press.

Howson, C., 2011, *A Just Church: 21st Century Liberation Theology in Action*, London: Bloomsbury.

Ivereigh, A., 2010, *Faithful Citizens: A Practical Guide to Catholic Social Teaching and Community Organising*, London: Darton, Longman & Todd.

Jaques, E., 1991, 'In Praise of Hierarchy', in G. Thompson, J. Frances, R. Levacic and J. Mitchell (eds), *Markets, Hierarchies and Networks: The Coordination of Social Life*, London: Sage, pp. 108–18.

Keen, R., 2014, 'Membership of UK Political Parties', *Commons Library Standard Note*, London: House of Commons.

King, A. and I. Crewe, 2013, *The Blunders of Our Governments*, London: Oneworld Publications.

Lipsky, M., 1980, *Street-Level Bureaucracy: Dilemmas of the Individual in Public Services*, New York: Russell Sage Foundation.

Lucas, C., 2012, *Social Politics: Political Campaigning in a Social Media Era*, Kindle.

McCracken, V. (ed.), 2014, *Christian Faith and Social Justice: Five Views*, London: Bloomsbury Academic.

Newman, I., 2014, *Reclaiming Local Democracy: A Progressive Future for Local Government*, Bristol: Policy Press.

Newman, J. (ed.), 2005, *Remaking Governance: Peoples, Politics and the Public Sphere*, Bristol: Policy Press.

Palmer, H., 1995, *The Enneagram in Love and Work*, NewYork: HarperOne.

Phillips, E., 2012, *Political Theology: A Guide for the Perplexed*, London: Continuum.

Reader, J., 2008, *Reconstructing Practical Theology: The Impact of Globalization*, Aldershot: Ashgate.

Richards, P., 2005, *Be Your Own Spin Doctor: A Practical Guide to Using the Media*, London: Politico's Publishing.

Riso, D. R. and R. Hudson, 1999, *The Wisdom of the Enneagram*, New York: Bantam.

Ritchie, A., C. Burbridge et al., 2013, *Just Church: Local Congregations Transforming their Neighbourhoods*, London: The Contextual Theology Centre.

Rogers, A., 2013, *Being Built Together: A Story of New Black Majority Churches in the London Borough of Southwark*, London: University of Roehampton.

Rogers, J., 2010, *Facilitating Groups: Getting the Best out of a Group*, Maidenhead: Open University Press.

Sagovsky, N., 2008, *Christian Tradition and the Practice of Justice*, London: SPCK.

Scott, P. and W. T. Cavanaugh (eds), 2004, *The Blackwell Companion to Political Theology*, Oxford: Blackwell Publishing.

Sedmak, C., 2003, *Doing Local Theology: A Guide for Artisans of a New Humanity*, Maryknoll, NY: Orbis Books.

Shakespeare, K., 2014, 'One Army? The Challenge of Unity and Diversity for Spiritual Life Development in a Global Denomination', *Practical Theology* 7:2, pp. 96–108.

Shannahan, C., 2014, *A Theology of Community Organising: Power to the People*, Oxford: Routledge.

Sheffield Fairness Commission, 2013, *Making Sheffield Fairer*, Sheffield: Sheffield City Council.

Shier-Jones, A., 2009, *Pioneer Ministry and Fresh Expressions of Church*, London: SPCK.

Singelis, N., 2013, *The Political Side of Social Media*, self-published on Kindle.

Slater, V., 2015, *Chaplaincy Ministry and the Mission of the Church*, London: SCM Press.

Smith, G., 2007, *A Short History of Secularism*, Basingstoke: I. B. Tauris Publications.

SROI Network, The, 2012, *A Guide to SROI*, London: The SROI Network.

Stoddart, E., 2014, *Advancing Practical Theology: Critical Discipleship for Disturbing Times*, London: SCM Press.

Stoker, G., 2006, *Why Politics Matters: Making Democracy Work*, Basingstoke: Palgrave Macmillan.

Storrar, W. F. and A. R. Morton (eds), 2004, *Public Theology for the 21st Century*, Edinburgh: T & T Clark.

Sweeney, J., C. Watkins et al., 2006, *Going Forth: An Enquiry into Evangelisation and Renewal in the Roman Catholic Church in England and Wales*, Cambridge: Von Hügel Institute and Margaret Beaufort Institute for Theology.

Taylor, C., 2007, *The Secular Age*, Cambridge, MA: Harvard University Press.

Thomas, S., 2013, 'Re-engaging with the Margins: The Salvation Army 614UK Network and Incarnational Practice', in P. Cloke, J. Beaumont and A. Williams (eds), *Working Faith: Faith-based Organisations and Urban Social Justice*, Milton Keynes: Paternoster, pp. 66–84.

Thompson, J. with S. Pattison et al., 2008, *SCM Studyguide to Theological Reflection*, London: SCM Press.

Volf, M., 2011, *A Public Faith: How Followers of Christ should Serve the Common Good*, Grand Rapids, MI: Brazos Books.

Wainwright, H., 2009, *Public Service Reform ... But Not As We Know It! How Democracy can Transform Public Services*, Hove: Picnic Publishing.

Walton, H., 2014, *Writing Methods in Theological Reflection*, London: SCM Press.

Widdicombe, C., 2000, *Meetings that Work: A Practical Guide to Teamworking in Groups*, Cambridge: Lutterworth.

Williams, R., 2012, *Faith in the Public Square*, London: Bloomsbury.

Wright, C. J. H., 2010, *The Mission of God's People*, Grand Rapids, MI: Zondervan.

Websites

Adjournment debates: www.parliament.uk/about/how/business/adjournment.

All Party Parliamentary Groups Register: www.publications.parliament.uk/pa/cm/cmallparty/register/contents.htm.

A Rocha: www.arocha.org.uk.

Charity trustees: www.gov.uk/charity-trustee-whats-involved.

Christians in Politics: www.christiansinpolitics.org.uk/.

Church Action on Poverty: www.church-poverty.org.uk.

Citizens Advice: www.citizensadvice.org.uk.

Faith-based Facilitation: www.salvationarmy.org/fbf.

Freedom of Information Requests: www.gov.uk/make-a-freedom-of-information-request/the-freedom-of-information-act.

An online tool for making freedom of information request: www.whatdotheyknow.com.

Hansard: www.parliament.uk/business/publications/hansard.

Housing Justice: www.housingjustice.org.uk.

Law centres information: www.lawcentres.org.uk.

Ombudsman: www.ombudsmanassociation.org/find-an-ombudsman.php.

Parliament at Westminster: www.parliament.uk.

Petitions: www.change.org. The site enables anyone, anywhere to start an online petition.

Regulators: discuss.bis.gov.uk/focusonenforcement/list-of-regulators-and-their-remit.

School governors: www.sgoss.org.uk.

Single person households: www.ons.gov.uk/ons/taxonomy/index.html?nscl=One-person+Households.

Street Life: www.streetlife.com.

Street Pastors: www.streetpastors.org.

They work for you: www.theyworkforyou.com.

Together for the Common Good: www.togetherforthecommongood.co.uk/home.html.

Tribunals: www.justice.gov.uk/about/hmcts/tribunals.

Write to them: www.writetothem.com.

Index of Authors

Atherton, J. 25
Baker, C. xiv, 127
Bennett, Z. 115
Bennett Moore, Z. 13
Bevans, S. 2, 11, 113
Bickley, P. 8
Bishop, G. 26
Bosch, D. J. 1
Bretherton, L. 1, 26, 127
Brown, M. 25, 127
Cameron, H. xvi, xviii, 34, 60, 61, 62, 115, 128
Catholic Bishop's Conference of England and Wales 35
Cavanaugh, W. T. 127
Chaplin, J. 25, 127
Crewe, I. 23
Davie, G. 1
Davis, A. 5
Gillham, B. 53
Graham, E. 24, 115, 127
Grey, C. 72
Hallsworth, M. 22, 23
Healthwatch England 108
Hebden, K. 26
Heywood, D. xvi
Hills, J. xii, 128
Hornsby-Smith, M. P. 70
Howson, C. 26
Hudson, R. 43
Ivereigh, A. 26
Jaques, E. 70
Keen, R. xii

King, A. 23
Lipsky, M. 55
Lucas, C. 102
McCracken, V. 5
Morton, A. R. 127
Newman, I. 6, 129
Newman, J. 6
Palmer, H. 43
Pattison, S. 128
Phillips, E. 126
Reader, J. 13, 128
Riso, D. R. 43
Richards, P. 101
Ritchie, A. 25
Rogers, A. x
Rogers, J. 41
Sagovsky, N. 3
Schroeder, R. P. 1, 113
Scott, P. 127
Shakespeare, K. 43
Shannahan, C. 26
Sheffield Fairness Commission 35
Shier-Jones, A. ix
Slater, V. x, 33
Smith, G. 127
SROI Network 89
Stoddart, E. 4
Stoker, G. xi, 128
Storrar, W. F. 127
Sweeney, J. ix
Taylor, C. 1
Thomas, S. 26
Thompson, J. 128

Volf, M. 17
Wainwright, H. 73, 129
Walton, H. 115

Widdicombe, C. 41
Williams, R. 4, 17
Wright, C. J. H. 3

Index of Subjects

accountability xi, 6–8, 17, 27, 90, 106–7
'Ask' 29, 32, 59–60, 77, 81–6, 93–4, 106
Authority 14, 16–20, 25, 28, 50, 52, 56, 60, 66, 68, 69–70, 72, 76, 77, 82–3, 86, 91, 94, 98, 100, 105–6

back office/ front office 72–3
bible 38, 43, 60–1, 66, 67, 112, 123–5
boundary-spanning 53

campaign 13, 19, 25–6, 47, 51, 89, 97–8, 102–3, 120
campaigning 15, 18, 47, 88, 94, 102, 118
case for support 84–6, 91, 93, 99, 103
charity law 117–18
chaplaincy x, xviii, 2, 33, 40
common good xiii, 4, 17, 25–6, 35, 134
community organizing 25
compassion 2, 3, 9, 11, 32–3, 115
conditionality 74–5
consultation 71, 81, 87, 88, 90–2
complexity xii–xiii, 77

data 52–4, 58, 79, 103, 107
democracy xi–xii, xvii, 27, 128–9
diaspora churches x
discretion xiii, 6–7, 15, 53, 55–6, 70–2, 74–5, 95, 98
discipleship 9, 112–13

electoral law 88, 117, 118–19
ethical 3, 25, 50, 51–2, 60, 100, 112
evangelization ix, x, xviii, 2, 33, 113
evaluating 29, 45, 47, 93, 104–110

family 3, 12, 38, 39, 116

good society 3–5

hope 9, 59, 62–5, 114
household 8–9, 11–13, 15, 51
human flourishing xiii, xiv, 27, 35–6, 61–3, 66, 128

influence 19–21, 23, 37, 75, 86, 88–90, 115, 117
integrated mission 11, 24, 26–7, 42, 114–15

kingdom 3, 62–5

law 88, 96, 117–20, 134
local authority 6, 54, 57, 90, 103
localism xii, 27, 68, 128

manifestos 87–8
market 5, 7, 63, 116
media (not social media) xi–xii,
    xvii, 4, 21, 23, 27, 66, 84–5,
    88, 96, 99, 100–1, 115
meetings xviii, 28, 41–2, 85–6,
    95

pastoral x, xv, xvi, xix, 2–3, 9,
    11–13, 28, 30, 33, 114
pluralism 17
policy xvi, xvii, 4, 6, 11, 17,
    20–4, 25, 55, 86, 88, 121
political cycle 86–90
political theology 126–7
practical theology xvi, xviii, xix,
    3, 11
public theology xv, 24, 115,
    126–8

radical 16–17, 24, 26
regulation xi, 18, 73
righteousness 2–3, 11, 32, 66,
    115

scrutiny xii–xiv, 13, 90
social action ix, x, xviii, 2, 7–8,
    11, 33
social media 84, 95, 99, 101–3
stakeholder analysis 36–7, 47,
    57, 82
state 4, 17, 27, 74
supply chain 75–6, 91

targets 55, 71, 74, 75
team xviii, 28, 29, 39–46, 50–4,
    56–7, 59–62, 76–8, 81–2, 84,
    86, 93–4, 100–2, 104–7, 110,
    112–13
tradition ix, xiv, xv, xvi, xviii,
    xix, 2, 4, 9, 29–30, 42, 44–6,
    59–61, 112, 114–15

unitary 16–17

visits 83–5
voluntary sector 6, 72

welfare state xiii, 6–7, 128
wicked problems 76–7